A Home In The Tall Marsh Grass

A HOME IN THE TALL MARSH GRASS

ROY ATTAWAY

Lyons & Burford, Publishers

Printed in the United States of America

10 9 8 7 6 5 4 3 2 1

Design by Howard P. Johnson

LIBRARY OF CONGRESS CATALOGING-IN-PUBLICATION DATA

Attaway, Roy.
    A home in the tall marsh grass / Roy Attaway.
      p. cm.
    Includes index.
    ISBN 1-55821-254-X : $18.95
    1. Attaway, Roy—Family relationships. 2. Journalists—United
States—Biography. 3. Editors—United States—Biography. 4. South
Carolina—Social life and customs. I. Title.
PN4974.A66A3   1993
070'.92—dc20   93-29940
[B]   CIP

For STORMY, CATHY, and BANKS,
who share his genes.
For ROBYN, who has heard the
stories a thousand times.
And for JANE,
who was witness to many.

1

During the latter years of World War II, we lived in the teacherage at Lobeco, South Carolina, where my mother had taken the position as principal of the elementary school for white children. Lobeco was a two-store, four-house community that owed its existence to the Seaboard Airline Railroad and a packing shed from which vegetables were shipped to northern markets. The railroad's main line ran through it like a zipper, stitching the crossroads together—the fields, the buildings, the woodlands—as if they would fly apart without it. Which, in fact, they nearly did. Years later, I would return to find the rails had been ripped out of the earth like the spine from some recumbent beast, leaving the hamlet formless and forlorn, not uninhabitable but uninviting, its purpose diminished, like a temporary wartime capital now forgotten save for a rusting, leaning historical marker that nobody stopped to read. In this case, there wasn't even a marker. For a time, though, it was the omphalus of the universe and the place where I learned to fish under the not-always-patient tutelage of my father.

Daddy was of medium stature, somewhere between 5'9" and 5'10", I'd guess, and—in the parlance of the Deep South—was known as Big Roy. Never mind that from age twelve on I stood over him by a good three inches. He was darkly complected, in contrast to my mother's (and my) fairness, became increasingly stooped as he aged, and was quick and nervous of gesture. He was gregarious and affectionate and quite popular with almost everyone he met, but from a very early time we were like those little black and white plastic Scotty dogs with the magnets glued to their bottoms: at a certain distance, we coexisted easily; face-to-face, we seemed to repel, sometimes with a nearly ugly vehemence, a context all the more disturbing, more agonizing, considering the love we craved from each other.

He brought us to Lobeco, which is on the mainland fringe of Beaufort County, in the summer of 1943. About a half a mile east of the railroad crossing, a sluggish tidal strait called Whale Branch cuts loose the major sea islands of the county: Port Royal (the largest and on which the county seat, Beaufort, is located), Lady's, and St. Helena, and the lesser ones with names like Seabrook, Morgan, Coosaw, Datha (now Dataw), Polawana, Cat, Parris (home of the United States Marine Corps Recruit Depot), Barnwell, Brays, Distant, Lemon, Spring, Callawassie, Pinckney, Hog, Bull, Savage, and many others. The barrier islands, the ones that shoulder the brunt of the Atlantic swell, are Hunting, Fripp, Pritchard's, Capers, St. Phillips, Bay Point, Hilton Head, and Daufuskie. There are, according to one source that bothered to attempt an enumeration, sixty-five in all. This does not take into consideration the hundreds of smaller ones—hummocks, really—some scarcely more than a spume of cedar and palmetto. They are all remnants of an Eocene ocean floor.

Two major sounds, St. Helena and Port Royal, and one smaller one, Calibogue, bring fresh seawater deeply into the archipelago. St. Helena Sound, the largest, narrows to become Coosaw River, while Port Royal Sound bifurcates into Beaufort River and Broad River. From these bodies, countless smaller rivers and creeks probe the soft, vulnerable isles like eager tendrils of an ocean bent on subduction of the continent.

The islands themselves are encircled (except on the ocean side of the barrier group) by passementeries of rich marshlands. The county is in the very southeasternmost corner of the state, a region known as the Lowcountry that presses on Georgia and almost succeeds in touching Florida. Millions of years ago, the Supercontinent was ripped apart by drifting tectonic plates, creating Gondwanaland and Laurentia—Africa and North America, respectively. Fossils of plants and animals deemed indigenous to Africa have been found embedded in South Carolina limestone. Imagine my shock twenty years ago when I stood on the deck of a sailing ship and got my first glimpse of The Dark Continent at the mouth of the Gambia River and found an unnervingly familiar landscape: the same wide, sandy beaches, the same tall dunes surmounted by pine and palmetto. Imagine, too, the reaction of slaves who came from the barracoons of Banjul to the plantation streets of the Lowcountry. It must have been a surprise. Perhaps they thought it was a cruel joke. Although, in their limited experience they simply may have thought this was the way the whole world looked.

In the eighteenth century, the American naturalist William Bartram traveled extensively through the Southeast and wrote with great affection for the Lowcountry:

> ". . . Nearly one third of this vast plain is what the inhabitants call swamps, which are the sources of numerous small rivers and their branches: these they call salt rivers, because the tides flow near to their sources, and generally carry a good depth and breadth of water for small craft, twenty or thirty miles upwards from the sea, when they branch and spread abroad like an open hand, interlocking with each other, and forming a chain of swamps across the Carolinas and Georgia, several hundred miles parallel with the sea coast. These swamps are fed and replenished constantly by an infinite number of rivulets and rills, which spring out of the first bank of ascent . . ."

It was, and is, despite heavy development in recent years, one of the last pristine estuarine areas on the Eastern Seaboard. For nearly five centuries—nearly two hundred centuries, if you count the pre-Columbian aboriginal inhabitants—various peoples have been seduced by this subtropical web of water and tenuous land. It was—and is—a wonderful place in which to grow up.

By an accident of fate, I had been born in Walterboro, in Colleton County—the next one inland, where the salt marsh gives way to the lush jungles of cypress and tupelo and the rivers run silkily, stained a deep tobacco by the tannic acid from tree roots. Both of my parents were from Beaufort County, but Daddy had moved his life insurance business to Walterboro in the early 1930s, seeking a larger, more active clientele. It helps to understand that prior to World War II, Beaufort—and most of its county—was isolated. There was only the one bridge, over Whale Branch, connecting the islands to the outside world. As recently as the 1950s, many of the islands, including Hilton Head, remained adrift from the mainstream of life. It is difficult to imagine that Hilton Head Island, its magnificent maritime forests now displaced by golf courses, tennis courts, condominiums, hotels and restaurants, as a place where Gullah—the English-based Sea Island creole—was the lingua franca even as television was beaming Uncle Miltie and Ed Sullivan into households a few miles away. Today, a Midwestern twang or latent Noo Yawkese is as apt to be heard as a drawl. The natives—who are as rare as native Manhattanites—occasionally vent their resentment. A favorite bumper sticker on the island proclaims: "I don't give a damn how you did it up north."

Beaufort is about a fifteen-mile detour off U.S. 17, at that time the major traffic corridor linking Florida with the Northeast, and only a few adventuresome tourists and those with connections to the Marine Corps ever made it. Walterboro, on the other hand, throve as a tourist stop midway between Charleston and Savannah. Today, the roles are somewhat reversed. Beaufort (still connected by only two bridges) is a much-written-about antebellum town, unscathed by war—civil or social—and as lovely as ever. Hilton Head Island, in terms of gross income and tax revenues, has become the tail wagging the dog. For a while, Walterboro was cut off, like an oxbow in a river, as U.S. 17 was moved east, to shorten it, and widened to four lanes. The routing of Interstate Highway 95 just west of the city resurrected Walterboro's fortunes a bit, but the hotels are now motels and the restaurants tend to be fast-food joints just off the exit ramps, far removed from the charming old town center with its Robert Mills–designed courthouse. (Mills, a South Carolina native, was a disciple of both Thomas Jefferson and Benjamin Latrobe and is best known as the architect of the Washington Monument and the Treasury Building—among other edifices—in Washington, D.C.)

It was to these islands in 1562 that the Huguenot leader Jean Ribaut brought a band of ex-soldiers, most of whom were arquebusiers, disguised as colonists. Historian D. D. Wallace wrote: "The notices of the expedition were a mixture of Protestant religious enthusiasm, French patriotism, and the ambition to gain wealth at the expense of Spain."

Sailing up from the St. John's River, his first landfall on May 1 of that year, Ribaut and his fleet recorded what the Spaniard Vásquez D'Ayllón already had discovered, that the area was salubrious in every way. The islands were low, densely forested, rife with game, and provided plenty of fresh water. On the back side of Hilton Head, where the tidal ranges are extreme, they could even careen and rummage their ships, gouging from the sodden planks the filth of months at sea. Moving into Port Royal Sound and up Broad River, Ribaut remarked in his diary that there was no ". . . fayrer or fytter place" and where ". . . without danger, all the ships of the world might be harbored."

He built a log blockhouse, chinked with clay, thatched with straw, and surrounded by a modest moat. It had ". . . 4 bastions and 2 bronze falconets and 6 iron culverins therein . . . "

Ribaut sailed confidently back to France, only to find the country embroiled in civil conflict. The colonists, expecting his rapid return, made no attempts to plant anything edible or otherwise plan for the future. Within six months, they had exhausted their stores and the hospitality of the local caciques, or Indian chiefs. In desperation, they built a boat of rough-hewn slabs, caulked it with moss and pitch, made a sail of their own extra clothing, and drifted eastward into tragedy. Becalmed and dying of thirst and hunger, they drew straws and one man killed himself that the others might feast on his body and survive. The next day they sighted land and were rescued by an English ship.

After several attempts by the Spanish, including the founding of Santa Elena along what is now the eighth fairway of the golf course on Parris Island, a colony that lasted for more than a decade (1566–76), the English finally found permanent settlement in the earliest years of the eighteenth century. In fact, the English colonist William Sayle had dallied at Port Royal in 1670 before moving up the coast to found Charles Town (Charleston) on a swampy point at the confluence of the Ashley and Cooper rivers.

What made Lobeco a crossroads was U.S. Highway 21, the federal road that begins in Cleveland, Ohio, and burrows its way down through the continent in a mostly southerly direction until it gets to South Carolina, where it heads straight for the sea. From Whale Branch, the highway spins out through the furrowed fields and the dense stands of pine that are interspersed with bays of oak and laurel and the occasional microswamp of bald cypress. It skirts the muddy flanges of creeks and rivers, eventually looping around and through Beaufort, leaves the town on the Lady's Island Bridge, and cuts pretty much straight across that eponymous landmass and St. Helena Island before crossing two other bridges and ending in the clacking shade of palmettos in the public parking lot of the state park at Hunting Island. Until fairly recently, it crossed Whale Branch (which connects the tips of Coosaw and Broad rivers) on a two-lane swing-span bridge that rarely opened save for an occasional shrimpboat. Nevertheless, the state was required to have a bridge keeper on call. He lived in a small frame house on the Seabrook Island side of the river and spent most of his days fishing from his low concrete charge. I don't recall his name, except that we called him The Old Man. A four-lane bridge crosses Whale Branch now, incorporating the older span.

Between trains and the random vehicular traffic, Lobeco was consumed by silence, an absence of sound so complete and unnerving that at times you could hear only the ringing in your ears. Now and then, a fly buzzed or a chicken squawked, and when a screened door slapped shut, the flat sound of wood on wood rang through the hamlet like a rifle shot. In such quiet, you could hear a vehicle approaching long before it emerged from the mirage where the concrete melted into the horizon. Farm vehicles came at a crawl, as if there were no place to go and all day to get there. Tourists came at a more rapid clip, sometimes slowing to eye the stores as possible oases. And you could always tell the cars loaded with young marines headed back to the base at Parris Island because they drove very fast, as if the crossroads were a peril, a flaming hoop to dash through. No matter what kind of vehicle it was, truck, car, or pickup, they all hit the railroad crossing with a sound like an eruption of tympani.

2

We came to Lobeco primarily because Daddy had temporarily forsaken the insurance business and taken a job as rents administrator for the Office of Price Administration in Beaufort. His duty was to make sure the local landlords didn't gouge the long-suffering young marines and their families. In other words, you could renovate your garage or chicken coop and rent it as an apartment if you liked, but you couldn't charge exorbitant rent. It did not make Daddy very popular in a county that had suffered egregious poverty since the dark days of Reconstruction and now suddenly sniffed the breeze of profit in a wartime economy. This critical need for housing was a blight that affected Beaufort for years after the war; many a handsome old mansion was summarily chopped up into apartments to accommodate the market.

Daddy's quotidian commute took him over the Whale Branch Bridge. The Old Man's success in catching speckled trout did not escape his attention. As a young man, Daddy had turned briefly away from the creeks and marshes and become a scratch golfer. His enduring ambition as a boy had been to play professional baseball—an unrequited passion transferred, with unfortunate result, to me. During the great hurricane of 1940, he suffered a coronary thrombosis while trying to chop away a chinaberry tree than had fallen against the Little House in Walterboro. He spent more than a year in the Veterans' Hospital in Columbia, and when he came back to us, it was with a renewed passion for fishing. Doctor's orders. I can't imagine what doctor, in what state of mind, prescribed fishing as an instrument of relaxation. Clearly, the doctor understood neither my father nor fishing.

With the acuity of middle age, I can recall in vivid detail events, conversations, of my earliest childhood, whereas the name and face of someone I met last week at a cocktail party have the clarity of newsprint on a wet sidewalk. Conversations with my parents are easy to re-create, even if I don't remember the exact words (which, in many instances I do) because I have only to listen to their voices, the cadences, in my mind, and know what they probably said.

There is a curious exception: the year Daddy spent in the Veterans' Hospital. I know he did, because I have been told many times that it was so. I have no recollection of it. It is as if slates had been rubbed and smeared to a chalky and unreadable state. By the same token, I can remember a number of things that were reinforced by the telling of them by my parents. But there are others of which they could have no knowledge because they either weren't there, or were so only peripherally. For example, I remember standing on tiptoe looking out a back window while my nursemaid dressed me in a pale green aviator's suit while watching my mother and other parents corral my coevals for my third birthday party. Everybody else was in white; the tablecloths were white, as were the cartons of ice cream and the cake (there are small, fuzzy black-and-white Kodak prints attesting to this, but no one photographed me in that back room). I remember running in a tangle of garden hose with my cousin, Jackie Summers, and falling against the brick steps, gashing my forehead. I still have a pale, lumpy cicatrix right under the hairline as a souvenir. I remember trying to find where the cat, Paderewski, covered its feces under the trees. I remember trying to dig a hole to China in the front yard (based on fallacious intelligence from my mother; I was far too young to understand that it was also facetious); sitting on the curb with books from my parents' shelves, pretending I was going to Walterboro High School across the street; and the police shooting a mad dog under a neighboring house. I remember the nursemaid taking me for an outing, buying razor blades and slipping them into her bra, and then parking me outside a grocery-cum-ginmill while she went in for a drink. I played in the dust—quite happily, I'm sure—with the dogs and an occasional curious black child.

All of this at what we called the Little House, where we lived first.

Later, we moved up Hampton Street to the Big House, a rambling two-story dwelling where mother took in boarders for a while, mostly young couples brought to Walterboro by the war. The husbands were attached to the nearby Army Air Corps field where crews for B–25 bombers were trained.

I remember Marion Sams eating mayonnaise sandwiches—and demanding the crust be cut off the bread. When that did not satisfy him (or me) we would go out back, where his father kept a kennel of bird dogs, and eat dog biscuits. I remember the lemonade stand Marion had and Glen Utsey teaching me the Pepsi-Cola jingle with the altered lyrics: "Pepsi-Cola burps a lot . . ." I recall my first pair of boots, knee-length, which I laced up sweatingly only to discover they were on the wrong feet. I remember listening to the *William Tell* Overture on our phonograph and telling my supremely irritated Aunt Gladys that I would come to bed as soon as Tonto rode in. I remember walking to Mrs. Fishburne's kindergarten wearing a bath towel around my neck and being teased by older boys. ("Look, he's wearin' his mamma's towel! He thinks he's Superman!") I remember the summer the polio epidemic confined me to the yard and I stood just inside the low brick wall, holding out a handful of copper pennies to the kind—if mock—admiration of passing adults. I will never forget sitting at the piano, plinking out some nonsensical tune and looking up to discover my mother standing a few feet away, holding a black-and-white stuffed panda.

But there is a gap of about a year. My father disappeared, and part of my life with it.

Daddy had been born not far from Lobeco in the seaport village of Port Royal on December 4, 1896. It was near the end of the tall-ships era, and vessels from all over the world stood for the little community's docks, taking on cargoes of cotton, naval stores, and phosphate. Politics has kept Port Royal from developing its potential as entrepôt, although the State Ports Authority did build a modest facility there in the 1950s—over the nearly-dead bodies of the Charleston lobby. Except for the notorious drifts of the southeastern bar at the entrance of Port Royal Sound, it is a fine natural habor, recognized and recorded as such more than 400 years ago by the intrepid Jean Ribaut. The village sits on a bluff overlooking Battery Creek, an arm of Beaufort River.

Port Royal grew because of its natural attributes and, despite Charleston's hegemony in colonial and federal affairs, the Charleston and Western Railroad eventually sent down a spur to accommodate commerce. By the late nineteenth century, Port Royal was a prosperous and promising place.

My grandfather, John Kansas Attaway, married the petite Laura Jane Bailey on December 27, 1888. They were both natives of Barnwell County, South Carolina, up the Savannah River. They came to the Lowcountry and settled in Port Royal. Laura Bailey bore him five sons and one daughter: John Kansas, Jr. (who died at the age of fifteen in 1905); the twins, Roy (my father) and Fred; Herbert; Jim (who died two days after my first birthday); and Annie Laurie. He was a successful merchant and planter, owning stores at Port Royal and Sheldon and farmed lands around Gardens Corner and Brays Island. He died in 1910, collapsing into my father's arms on the railroad platform at Sheldon as they waited for the train to Port Royal.

Before this disaster, my father and his siblings enjoyed the privileges of modest wealth and the glories of a Lowcountry still teeming with fish and game. They fished from the docks, handlining for sheepshead among the pilings or casting shrimp against the marsh fringe for spottail bass and speckled trout. Once, Daddy and Fred held an impromptu swimming race across a creek, and both crashed into the corpse of a dead Negro. Crabs were feasting on the pitiful remains. I have often wondered whether this played a role in his passing estrangement from the marshes he loved so well—or whether that had been simply a natural young-adult disavowal of boyish and natal passions.

In World War I, Daddy enlisted in the United States Navy and served aboard a warship. He was stationed in Charleston, and his ship took him at least once to New York. He saw no military action, but acquired a formidable vocabulary of swear words.

By 1927, the empire was gone. The Deep South suffered a severe economic depression two years prior to the crash on Wall Street. The stores, the lands, were no longer family held. Over the next decade, the family dispersed: Fred moved to Charleston and became the Sinclair Oil distributor; Herbert was elected as County Road Supervisor; Jim died; Annie Laurie married and moved to Augusta; and Daddy drifted into the insurance and real-estate business.

In 1928 he married Claire Evangeline Walker of Hardeeville, S.C., in a ceremony on Buckfield Plantation. I came much later—nine years, to be exact. I was a complete surprise. Many mothers think their children are godsends. Mine thought I was a miracle. It is a burden no child should bear. My father was forty-one when he sired me. Eventually, they moved to Walterboro, but I know that his spirit, like mine, was truly at peace only in the creeks and marshes of Beaufort County.

3

f memory serves, however, the first fish I ever caught were under the loving eye of my maternal grandfather, Charles Albert Martell Walker. He was the son of Edwin A. Walker, a schoolmaster who ran a private academy near Whitehall, in Colleton County. His grandfather, Daniel Walker, a millwright, had come over from near Glasgow in the early 1800s to build sluice gates for the rice plantations. Great-granddaddy Edwin had married Rebecca Benton, whose family lived on parcels of land originally granted by the Crown. He was a scholarly man, supposedly fluent in Latin and Greek. He was sucked into the maelstrom of the War Between the States, as were all the others of his generation. I still have a letter he wrote, in a most elegant handwriting, on Christmas Day, 1861, as his company bivouacked near Pocotaligo, waiting for the Yankees to attack. (Surely he could not have envisioned that, a century later, great convoys of them would race down I–95 right by this very battlefield in a far-more-benign invasion.) I also have the small cast-iron pot he carried to cook his meals in. Mother used it for years as a doorstop.

Granddaddy—Mr. Cholly to most people in the county—

was a tall, rawboned man with a woodsman's loping stride and a disposition as sweet as the yellow jasmine that entwined the fence. It was said that he once worked as a riverboat gambler—a piece of family lore as musty and suspect as any—but he did have a penchant for gambling, which he displayed so disastrously. He made a fortune in timber and turpentine. It it said that he once owned the largest sawmill east of the Mississippi. He married Edith Stuart of Oatmeal, Texas (whom he had met in Florida), and brought her back to Hardeeville, then in Beaufort County, where his business flourished on the edge of the great Savannah River Swamp. For a time, he was in partnership with a Mr. Johnson, and they had offices on Factors' Walk in Savannah, where they were indeed factors.

Unfortunately, his favorite pasttime was to lease a private railroad car and go off for days at a time with his cronies, gambling and drinking good whiskey. He lost the first fortune. He built another. And he lost that, too. It is also said that he owned a hotel in Savannah and lost that on the turn of a card. Grandmother Edith left him, taking the children to Charlotte, North Carolina.

Their departure clearly dispirited him. He retired to Colleton County to live with his sister and a maiden cousin in the small frame house that he, his brother David, and their father had built after Lee surrendered and the Confederates drifted back to the conflagrant ruins. It was in this house that I first knew him.

The house had three bedrooms, a living room, and a detached kitchen connected by a short breezeway—a style of architecture common to grand houses and poor ones alike in that the threat of fire from the kitchen was held at bay from the principal dwelling. There was a front porch and an outhouse. There was a barn and a well from which all drinking and bathing water was drawn by hand. The house sat on a knoll that sloped away to the dark swamps of a creek called Sandy Run. In front of the house was a trace begun by Indians and widened and deepened by traffic over millennia. When Sherman's army drove from Atlanta to the sea (at Savannah), it then split into two arms and wheeled into South Carolina. One force entered Beaufort by water; the other crossed the

Savannah River some 30 miles above that city. Feinting simultaneously toward Charleston and Augusta to confuse the Confederates and divide their resistance, Sherman then plunged into the heart of the hated state (South Carolina had led the way toward secession), driving toward Columbia with the combined force. Elements of the Beaufort column passed along this trace, the closest thing then to a highway. Every town along the way was sacked and burned: Hardeeville, Grahamville, McPhersonville, Barnwell, Blackville, Midway, Orangeburg, and Lexington. He savored the destruction of Columbia, although he claimed he had no direct hand in it. (The city surrendered to him; the burning began several days later when word spread through his occupying army that it would please their general if they did so.) The arson was vicious and indiscriminate, although the capitol was spared, as were a few houses and buildings of architectural merit (Robert Mills's at the University of South Carolina among them). For this reason, downtown Columbia, like downtown Atlanta, is largely bereft of any real architectural heritage; most things there seem indeterminate and awkward and the newer buildings, the sharp-edged modern ones, only add to the sense of displacement.

The original house in which my great-grandparents lived was a few miles away and had burned by accident, not by the Yankees. Nevertheless, Sherman's scorched-earth policy swept away even the last chicken. All that survives are a few silver serving spoons that great-grandmother buried in the yard. Family legend has it that she scolded the Yankee captain who raided the farm, but I suspect they took everything anyway.

It was only logical that when the family rebuilt, they chose a site nearer the trace, as was the custom. Every passerby, even a stranger, was a source of news and gossip and not to be missed. Information was exchanged for hospitality, and vice versa.

My parents began depositing me here from about age four, no doubt to gain respite from the energetic chaos I generated. We also held family reunions there for a time, the clans gathering at Easter for services at Black Creek Church. The traditional egg hunt followed, an antic scramble of cousins through hedges and fences, under the house, around tree roots and potato safes, by the well and in the barn. The prize for the golden egg was a Whitman Sampler of chocolates. I never won it and I've never forgotten it (or, obviously, gotten over it) either.

Mr. Cholly was a doting grandfather. If I had asked for the watch he carried on a fob, he would have given it to me. As it was, he took me everywhere with him. When the household needed supplies from the crossroads store, some three or four miles distant, he would hitch up the wagon and he and I would ride side by side, smoking pipes. He taught me how to pack a pipe well so you could smoke it upside down in the rain. When he had bought the flour and salt, or whatever it was that was required, he would buy himself a bottle of beer and we would share that, too, on the ride home. In the evenings, he listened to the news on his brown Philco radio and then read to me from *The Arabian Nights*. He always smelled richly of Half & Half tobacco and Octagon soap. And afterward, we would wash our feet and go to sleep in the front bedroom, he in one bed, and I in another. When the panther screamed in the swamp, a horrible sound like a woman suffering indescribable pain, he would say softly in the darkness: "It's all right, darlin'. He won't get you." He kept a double-barreled shotgun over his bed and a mean yellow cur named Mike slept on the porch, sometimes arousing the household with his deep barking when deer would sneak into the yard for the crabapples.

Despite his fall from grace, Granddaddy never lost his sense of humor. He once convinced one of the bomber crews boarding with us in Walterboro to drop a practice bomb on the farmstead as a joke. The bomb, filled with some white substance for marking on the bombing range, detonated on the fields below the house. He roared with laughter when he told the story—often—of how this hellish war machine circled the house and then came in at treetop level to loose its ersatz instrument of destruction. His sister, Great Aunt Dessie, ran from the kitchen, shrieking: "The Russians has riz! The Russians has riz!"

In the langorous cool of a Lowcountry summer morning, we would be awakened by the coarse croakings and cracked shrills of a bantam rooster perched in the low-slung branches of the live oak. This dissonant aubade soon would be followed by the sounds of Aunt Dessie stirring the coals in the wood stove. Granddaddy would rise slowly and dress with deliberation, slipping short, clocked socks over his bony feet, and then pulling on the rough cotton trousers with their suspenders, and then a collarless shirt. Last, he would put on the black shoes he always wore. He did this with the quiet dignity of a lord justice dressing for court. I, meanwhile, would jump out of bed and put on a pair of khaki shorts. Nothing more. We would then go to the front porch, away from the women, and pee off the edge where rain from the gutterless tin roof had carved narrow channels in the white sand, antediluvian beach sand. We then washed our hands in the enameled washbasin on the breezeway and entered the kitchen, redolent of coffee and bacon and of biscuits baking.

At breakfast, he would sip his coffee, stained brown by cream from the cow and sweetened with homemade molasses. I had my cup, as well. Aunt Dessie or Cousin Lalie (Eulalie) would serve him clabber, a sour-tasting, yogurtlike curdled milk, on which he doted. This was a rare departure from our singularly bonded activity. (I was his shadow.) I never developed a taste for it and ate, instead, the bacon and hominy and biscuits spread with freshly churned butter and fox-grape jelly.

By now the sun would be tangled in the canopy of the forest and, as we ate the last of our breakfast, he would ask what I wanted to do for the day.

"Can we go fishin'?"

"Of course, darlin'."

It was a ritual, enacted with great solemnity on his part, shy impatience on mine.

We would then go to the outhouse to do our manly duties. We sat over the reeking pit, Granddaddy smoking his first pipe of the day (a nearly-adequate air freshener) and reading the Time magazines my father brought him. When he was finished with both sides of a page, he would carefully tear it out and place in it a pile for more utilitarian purposes. I chose an out-dated Sears, Roebuck & Company catalog.

At last he would collect the supple bamboo fishing poles from the rafters under the porch roof, and we would head off in tandem down the umbrageous tunnel of the trace toward the run. Granddaddy led. I followed, skipping to keep pace. In early summer, there were blackberries on which I might snack en route—and which we would later pick for pies.

"Be careful, darlin', and walk in the middle . . ."

"Yessir."

He had taught me about the snakes, the diamondback and timber rattlers that glided through the grasses in search of small rodents. There were cottonmouth moccasins in the run, too, and I had seen those on occasion. But they never kept me from swimming where the waters spilled like thin red wine over the white sand bottom of the trace and then swirled into a bankside hole.

Where the grasses had not yet been touched by the sun, he would stop and probe carefully and snatch up the grasshoppers still laden with dew and clumsy. These he would put into a jar with holes punched in its lid. Sometimes we used earthworms dug from the damp soil around the well or under the leaf mold, or crickets trapped in the barn.

When we came to the run, he would walk slowly along the path which was eroded, like the trace, by generations of cautious feet. He held the poles backward, the easier to thread them through the brush and trees, and he used these butt ends to switch against the grass for snakes. Thus we would descend from the sandy hills, the ancient dunes, and enter the swamp.

"Now, be quiet, darlin'."

"Yessir."

Not too many miles from this very spot, one of the Lowcountry's aristocratic colonial landowners built a fine brick hunting lodge. He called it his Temple of Sport. (The outlines of its foundations are still discernible on the forest floor only a few yards off Highway 17.) The swamp, the graceful natural nave of trees, was ours. We followed the rises, a patchwork of unsubstantial earth lashed together by sinuous roots, through dew-diamond webs, whispering canebrakes, and jungles of feathery fern that were pleasant to my bare feet. The trees were lianastrung and tasseled with Spanish moss. At night it was, in my febrile imagination, a Piranesian nightmare where luminous h'ants drifted, their incorporeal forms slipping through solid trunks, and tormented souls moaned in agony. In the rising warmth of day, it was forest primeval, green and cool, where warblers flitted through the branches and the dull hammerings of the magnificent pileated woodpeckers echoed.

When we came to the place he reckoned best, Granddaddy would raise a hand and we would crouch and sneak closer to the brink. The run had become an inky lake, fanning out through the cypress knees, the channel all but imperceptible.

"See that pike yonder?" He took the pipe from his mouth and used the stem as a pointer.

"Yessir."

There was a small bulge in the water where a chain pickerel cruised. From time to time, the glassine surface was marred by the infinitesimal dapple of a feeding redbreast.

He baited the hook on my line.

"Now, darlin', swing the pole easy and drop your bait over near that log."

"Yessir."

My attempts were clumsy, hasty, often disastrous, but despite this, we always came away with a stringer of fish, mostly his, I'm sure. But the sudden plop of a grasshopper on the taut skin of the swamp was too much for any jittery, justifiably paranoid, but hungry fish. The sunfish were small, but feisty. The tips of our cane poles juddered with their attacks. I never caught a pickerel, but Granddaddy did now and then, and the quietude of the swamp was shattered by the violent, thrashing struggle.

When we had caught enough for dinner—the midday meal in the Lowcountry—we would go back to the place where the trace crossed the run, and I would splash about in the hole while he sat on the bank and smoked and watched.

Nearly a half-century later, I went back to the house, now owned by cousins. It had been abandoned long before and a new brick dwelling had been built by my second cousin, Cyril

Walker and his wife Geneva, nearer the highway—which parallels the trace. The old place still stood, not even appearing to be especially rickety. It was filled with farm implements. The roof over the back bedroom, Aunt Dessie's room, had partly caved in so that the rain fell in a straight line across the foot of her bed. The covers and the mattress had rotted down to the bedsprings precisely along the course of the rain. Above that, toward the headboard, the bed was still as neatly made as the day she died. I found a book with my mother's name inscribed on the flyleaf. Granddaddy's radio still stood in the corner by the fireplace. He had been dead for nearly four decades.

4

My *father never* thought much of canepole fishing. It is safe to assume that he did it as a child around Port Royal and Sheldon. But, by this time, wartime, the time I began to fish with Granddaddy, my parents had turned away from any such rusticity and found the bright promise of twentieth-century Frigidaire-Ford-electric range-and picture-show, Middle-Class America. Daddy was progressive—as a fisherman, anyway. He embraced the art of the artificial, spending hours on the riprap at Whale Branch, snapping out a small wooden, red-headed plug with two treble hooks. This seemed to satisfy the sportsman in him. When he was successful, he would hold up the trout or puppy drum with a grin and flip his false teeth around in his mouth (a talent I greatly admired). When he snagged the plug on the tough marsh stems or lost it to an oyster bed, he stamped around in a torrent of profanity. He also never made the connection between saltwater and corrosion. When he was through fishing for the day, he would lay the rods and reels in the trunk of the car and then wonder, two days later, why they were frozen. The makers of such obviously inferior fishing gear were immediately and everlastingly consigned to a special inferno.

Occasionally, we went back to the house on Sandy Run. Mother tended the graves at Black Creek, and we picnicked along the banks of one of the larger streams. Daddy gave me a canepole and a can of earthworms, but he stood pretty much apart, preferring to cast and retrieve his artificials—until and unless the fish began to bite, in which case he would hastily abandon sport for the sake of sport and join me. In such events, he would then scale and gut the iridescent panfish, and Mother would dredge them in flour and fry them in bacon grease in a heavy skillet over the coals of our campfire. But it was not to her liking. She wanted something that was more out of *House & Garden* than *Field & Stream*. More often, on these picnics, we ate grilled steak.

The first summer in Lobeco was a foretaste of the next three to come: barefoot adventures through the fields, the woodlands, and the marshes. Those selfsame bare feet more often than not were empurpled by potassium permanganate to kill ringworm. Mother would not let me go barefoot until the first of May, from which point I never wore shoes again until school started.

The Johnson family lived next door to the teacherage, but their son, Grady Byers, was older and mostly away at military school. The Wilsons lived down by the railroad and their son, Harry, Jr., who was a year younger than I, eventually became a good friend. But the closest family, and one with a boy my age, was a Negro family that lived in an unpainted shack directly across the highway. That first summer, their son, Bubba, was hired by my parents to be my playmate. They paid his family fifty cents a week. Bubba was a placid boy, good-natured, inquisitive, a good foil for my bossiness.

For about a year, Bubba and I were the closest of companions. We went everywhere together, playing soldier (mason jars filled with water and tied to our belt loops with string were our "canteens"), scooping up tadpoles from rain-swollen ditches, and hiding under a blanket by the front door where we could watch the lightning and hear the rain and feel safe at the same time when thunderstorms shook the teacherage. When I went to stay for a few days with my grandfather, Bubba came along and slept on a pallet on the floor at the foot of my bed. It was from Bubba, as much as anyone—including my father and a succession of friends, yardmen, and maids—that I learned to speak Gullah.

Eventually, Bubba and his family moved to a new house near Dale, too far for easy intercourse, and he slowly vanished from my life. I never even knew what his last name was, or if I did, I have forgotten it. And of that I am ashamed.

The slack was taken up by Little Harry Wilson and—when he was home—Grady Byers Johnson. Little Harry and I had much in common: an absolute knack—a genius, if you will—for getting into trouble. The Wilson's store was fertile ground for children with imaginations like Harry's and mine. We played hide-and-seek through its many chambers, including the Wilson's apartment upstairs. We spent endless hours in the cotton annex, a room attached to the store where farmers stored their unginned cotton awaiting transport. When the room was full, you could swan-dive from the rafters into the dusty white mound. We ran errands to earn pennies for candy and parched peanuts and sat on the tailgate of Mr. Wilson's pickup truck as he drove slowly down the rutted roads delivering groceries. Little Harry had a goat cart and a billygoat to pull it and we exhausted the pitiful animal, racing around the store, a lilliputian chariot driven by mad midgets. We built fires in the ditch behind the store over which we roasted potatoes or whatever else we thought needed cooking, including processed luncheon meats like baloney. We were "camping." But the fire was the thing; the lovely lambent flame was its own excuse for being. Somehow, we did not believe that the smoke would betray us. We were warned away from the riverbank, but of course we went there anyway, catching fiddler crabs in the high sand and chasing larger blue crabs in the shallows. Mud was our betrayer here, the smudges of it undeniable on our feet. For these and many other transgressions, we were punished. Harry, Sr., exacted immediate retribution. It was my doleful duty to go home, honor bound to inform my parents of our misdeeds, and then to be sent out into the edge of the woods to cut a switch for my own pain and suffering. The anticipation of the stinging lash usually was worse than the actuality. Or is that rationalization?

But it was the older boy, Grady Byers, who led me into the marsh.

A two-rut sandy and overgrown road ran down the eastern part of the Johnsons' property. It wound through stands of pines deep in broom sedge, through thickets of wild plums and bays of cassina. Eventually it led to the low ocher bluff crumbling into the edge of a creek. There was a boat there, a cypress bateau homemade on one of the islands, tethered to a root abandoned to the air by the receding sand. It probably belonged to a local fisherman. We used it as our warship, our crabbing and fishing boat, our diving platform. We never bothered with bathing suits. They would have give away our game, anyway, had we taken them home sopping wet. We swam in the altogether, and Grady Byers "taught" me to swim by throwing me out of the boat. It was a poor beginning. Even now, the best I can muster is a flailing dog paddle or a very inept and exhausting crawl.

Daddy caught us once. We were walking back home when we spotted the Ford coming slowly toward us down the ruts, plowing like an icebreaker through the billowing brown sedge. We were scolded. I was punished. But we went back. The creeks and marshes were a part of me already. Standing there, where ". . . The sun is a-wait at the ponderous gate of the West . . . " as the Georgia poet Sidney Lanier wrote ("The Marshes of Glynn"), I inhaled the profound richness, a pungency that suffused my very being. When the tide drops, it exposes broad flats of purple-brown pluff mud, nutrient-rich deltas denticulated here and there with outcroppings of oyster shells. In spring and early summer, the marsh grass bristles the river edges like a bright green crew cut. In winter it turns golden like fields of oats or rye and undulates in the wind, a sea of subtle and casual violence. When the sun heats the exposed flats, the gases trapped in them expand and burst through the surface in loud pops. Where the gases escape, there are holes in the flats like the top side of a half-done griddle cake. Here and there, the marshes are split by the creeks that alternately flood and drain them. As the water sinks from the roots of the grass to join the river's rush to the sea, it flickers and sings and the soft banks are branded by the triton tracks of shorebirds hunting minnows and larval shrimp. When the tide brims the grass, the creeks and rivers are serene, complacent mirrors to the sky with no hint of drama. As the waters recede, hiding places disappear, escape routes narrow, options vanish. Then the marshes come alive with the stalk of the hunter and the manic dash of the hunted. The seas of grass that tip above the flooding ocean's edge are at once a nursery and a killing field.

Each year, in late October or early November, the first cold fronts push down through the Lowcountry torpor and, as the water temperature in the creeks drops, the speckled trout (the spotted weakfish, *Cynoscion nebulosus*) come in with the tides to feed. There is a danger to the fish later in the brief winter if an early and bitterly cold front plunges the temperature of these relatively shallow waters too quickly. The trout are immobilized and are easy prey. I'm sure the Indians took advantage of it. In the mid-twentieth century, Lowcountry natives would back their cars and pickup trucks down to the water's edge and scoop up the stunned fish, like bears in Alaska. It happens only rarely, and nowadays it is illegal to take them that way. But, after the cold snaps, there was some remarkable trout fishing to be had off the riprap at the western end of the Whale Branch Bridge.

My father began to fish in earnest, a pattern he would follow for the rest of his life. After the war, be became quite ingenious about it. He bought a war-surplus Army field jacket and pants—both many sizes too big—and galoshes. As he drove around the counties on his insurance-sales rounds and found himself with a half-hour to spare, he would hasten to the nearest creek, put the oversized clothing on over his business suit, and fish. He kept minnow traps secreted in culverts all over the county, so fresh bait was never a problem. He never made much money, but we lived on a fairly healthy diet. Now and then he would burst into the kitchen at night, brandishing a stringer of trout or bass, as proud of himself as if he'd just delivered a life-insurance payment to some grateful family.

In the fall of 1943, I began my formal education at Lobeco Elementary, an event I had awaited with considerable enthusiasm. I could not wait to learn to read. I already could, in a simple way.

5

Lobeco was an expedient for my parents, a compromise, an interregnum to be endured as we slowly made our way back to their Beaufort, the end of our quiet little family diaspora in sight. To me, Lobeco was a grand place to live. The freedom granted by the country suited my explosive energy, my nonconformist (even then) persona, my capacity for getting into trouble. Once at the Big House in Walterboro, I had, in the short span of a few disastrous minutes, discovered a cache of discarded razor blades and the rubber mat from the trunk of Daddy's car, which he had washed and draped over the fence to dry. How easily it sliced! I also discovered that a garden hose turned on full blast could be induced to burrow itself underground—and very quickly. At Lobeco, I stuck a bent paper clip into a wall socket in order to power a "motor" I had built of my wooden Tinker-Toys. Clearly, those who tolerated me then (and now) are marked for early beatification.

I never noticed the hamlet's quasi-isolation. It was, I suppose, a classic case of not missing what you never knew.

But there were portents that something was askew, that our particular orbit yawed badly.

The teacherage was hearth and home. It was a four-bedroom, two-bath house with a small lending library attached to the eastern end. We occupied most of it, but two of the bedrooms were supposed to be quarters for unmarried teachers. To my recollection, there was only one young woman who stayed with us the entire time we lived there. The other teachers were married (all were women). Aunt Gladys, Mother's youngest sister, lived there for a time, too, and her boyfriend Harry, who was a B–25 pilot at the Army Air Corps base in Walterboro (was it Harry who dropped the "bomb" on Sandy Run? I rather think so), gave me my first watch and taught me to tell time. Harry also once gave me, for my birthday, a football and a basketball—both of which looked more than slightly used. I think Harry may have been a wizard at the military art of the midnight requisition.

We had a chicken yard out back, along with a small toolshed where my father raised biddies in a special incubator. The peeping yellow chicks arrived by parcel post in a cardboard box punched with airholes. Mother could clean and cook a chicken, but could not bear to kill them. The maid always had to do it. Sometimes the coup de grâce was instantaneously fatal; at others, the beheaded body would run in crazed circles, blood spurting from the neck stump. Hence the expression: "Running around like a chicken with its head cut off." I have witnessed it many times.

There was a large pine tree at either end of the house and, once, sitting with my parents in the living room during a violent thunderstorm, a bolt of blue lightning crackled from tree to tree, leaving a sulfurous wake through the house.

"That's the smell of Hell," my mother said.

And, truly, there was peril at hand. She once killed a diamondback rattler at the foot of the kitchen steps.

There also was opportunity: I was paid a penny for every fly I killed in the house. I would stalk them with a swatter and collect them in a mason jar. I learned quickly, in the spirit of nascent entrepreneurship, that an open-back screen door increased my chances for profit immeasurably.

The living room was also where we learned of the death of Franklin Delano Roosevelt. My mother was listening to the radio. Suddenly a siren wailed and an announcer told us the news. Mother screamed. She thought we surely would lose the war in Europe now.

This was where the sheriff called one day to tell Mother that Gladys had committed suicide. She had followed Harry to Washington, only to be dumped by him.

It was where we learned of the death of Aunt Midge Summers in Savannah. She had been very frail—a terrible asthmatic—and left three children, my cousins Bennie, Helen, and Jackie.

It was where I sat huddled ear-to-radio, listening to Santa Claus on WSAV in Savannah, praying for my name to be read, too. (It was.) It was where I figured out that Santa in no way could accomplish his mission with a mere sleigh and reindeer (it almost never snowed in the Lowcountry, anyway). No. Unquestionably, he used a helicopter.

It was where one evening Mother rose suddenly at the dinner table and hurled dishes against the wall. Ostensibly, her rage was the result of my whining. Over what? The food? She was a remarkable cook. I don't know. I doubt if I ever will. Like my father's disappearance from my orbit, it is something that remains buried. At this distance in time, the pain stems not so much from trying to sort truth from fantasy as in attempting to recognize truth itself.

Within a week of that dreadful evening, Daddy drove Mother and me to the railroad station at Yemassee, where the Atlantic Coast Line trains hurtled through, New York to Miami. It was raining when we left and quite late, well past my bedtime. I was excited, but disturbed. Something was quite wrong. I lay with my cheek against the cold pane. Rain mottled the glass and the landscape, gray and monotonous, was broken up by this imperfect lens into dots, like the pointillist paintings Mother had shown me in books. The fields were barren and soaked, water lying in vast, shallow lakes across the furrows, the treeline an encroaching smudge of black. We passed country stores where a single bulb shone over the stoop. The pathetic light made each store seem even more forlorn, an outpost in a bleak and forbidding world. Lights from the infrequent oncoming vehicles blinded us and then were gone. Daddy lit one of his Philip Morris cigarettes and opened the vent a crack to let the smoke escape.

"Daddy?"

"Yes, darlin'?"

"When I'm twenty-one, you know what I want for my birthday?"

"What's that?"

"A carton of Philip Morris and a cigarette lighter."

My father laughed. Mother made a derisive sound, like a deer snorting. She had said nothing since supper. They did not speak again until we got to the outskirts of Yemassee, another hamlet, but bigger than Lobeco. There were four or five stores, a bank, a café-cum-bus stop, and the railroad station. It was a fairly big station, with a white-painted barracks behind it. A sign outside said United States Marine Corps in Chinese red and gold. The barracks was a way station for young recruits who came down the ACL mainline from all over the East and Midwest. Yemassee was famous, Daddy said. You could walk into the Pennsylvania Railroad Station in New York City and ask for a ticket for Florence or Sumter, and the ticket agent would have to look it up; but if you asked for a ticket to Yemassee, his fingers flew right to it.

We parked behind the station and dashed through the rain to the Whites Only waiting room. Daddy carried both of our suitcases. The station smelled of heating oil from the stove at one end. The ticket office was in the middle, and through it I could look into the coloreds' waiting room: Negro men and women asleep on the wooden benches. Large ladies surrounded by boxes and suitcases tied with string; old men in suits that hung about their shoulders as if the fabric had given up hope of a fit.

Daddy bought the tickets while I stood on tiptoe at his

elbow. He gave them to Mother, who put them in her purse. We all sat down and he lit another cigarette.

"Don't do that," Mother said. Her eyes looked red and dull. She had spent much of the past two days in the bedroom, crying.

Daddy got up and walked out onto the platform. I followed, more awake than ever, excited by the prospect of sleeping and eating on a train. I had never even ridden on one before. Daddy put a nickel into a glass-bowled vending machine and shook out a handful of red, salted Spanish peanuts. He poured half of them into my hands. Light from the station streaked away down the burnished rails and across the track we could see the blurred figures moving behind the windows of the café. All of the other buildings were dark. It was raining harder and gray veils of water drifted past the lights. Daddy looked drawn and tired.

"Daddy?"

"Yes, son?"

"Why ain't you coming with us?"

"Aren't."

"Aren't."

"Momma needs a vacation."

"Will you come down, too?"

"Maybe. Maybe I'll just see you back here."

"You goin' fishin'?"

He smiled and put his hand on my head.

"Probably."

"Will you take me someday?"

He looked as if he might cry.

"Yes."

The Silver Meteor came into the station with an expanding roar, a sleek new diesel-electric engine heading a long line of shiny passenger cars. The ground and the building shook when the engine rumbled by. It stopped a good way down the tracks, and the doors on several of the cars opened and steps dropped to the platform with resounding clangs. Negro trainmen in vested suits and hard pillbox hats stepped into the steam. We went inside and got Mother and the suitcases, which Daddy handed to one of the porters. My parents said good-bye with perfunctory kisses. Daddy hugged me and kissed me and told me to take care of Mother. I watched him through the window of our Pullman sleeper. He stood at the edge of the platform and waved until we pulled away, gathering speed, and he was gone again.

I slept in the same berth with my mother that night. Our toiletries and incidentals swung in a net hammock overhead. When we awoke, Mother said we were in Florida. It looked no different from the Lowcountry. I was disappointed and I thought about my father.

All that day we continued down the peninsula, and gradually the landscape began to transform. The live oaks and stands of tall pine gave way to scrub and finally there were palm trees, regal things much taller than the native palmetto in South Carolina. It was sunny and the architecture seemed to reflect its influence. There were the cracker houses with their all-too-familiar screened porches and pitched tin gables, but I began to notice buildings of stucco with red terra-cotta tile roofs.

We stayed a few days in Miami with a cousin. I recall little about that, except going shopping with Mother for a bathing suit and several pair of short pants to replace the corduroy knickers I had worn on the train. I do remember the strand at Miami Beach, the water far more brilliant than our darkling seas.

Eventually, we moved on to stay with my maternal great-grandmother in Homestead. I was bored. She lived in a small bungalow, the chief attraction of which was an orange tree in the backyard. This was sufficient novelty to occupy me for a day or so. The best part was I could go barefoot—and it was February.

I wrote to Daddy:

> Homestead, Fla
> Feb. 9, 1945
>
> Dear Pop
> Mom says she wishes I was back in Lobeco because I want to spend too much money. Pop please help

me out and send me a little more cash because I have a
bout [sic] spent the $2.00 that you gave
I am having a good time but I miss you so much
love,
Son

He hated being called "Pop"! Once, on the way into Beaufort, we had given a lift to several young marines. One of them
said something like "Hey, Pop . . . "

"Don't call me 'Pop!'" my father snarled back.

He wrote Mother on Valentine's Day, saying that he had
sent us both cards for that occasion and acknowledging my
letter and promising to write to me. He also said he was trying
to get away to come join us.

And then we took the bus to Key West, to stay with my
Great Aunt Julia. She had a two-story house at 729 Truman
Avenue. The house had piazzas across the front and a deep,
lush garden. It is still there, in the guise of a bed-and-
breakfast—and looks quite wonderful, just as I remembered
it. Unfortunately, it was also home to my younger cousin Patsy,
Aunt Julia's ward. She grew up to be an astonishingly beautiful
woman, but at that stage I thought she was an insufferable
pest.

Key West, though, I found most attractive. We went to
the turtle kraals and ate turtle steak at a hotel. We ate Cuban
sandwiches in open-air cafés, served by swarthy waiters in
scarlet sashes. I swam on the one beach that was not coated
with oil—the residue of German submarine activity in the
shipping channels. The water, where it was not befouled,
shaded from pale aquamarine to deepest cobalt blue and
sometimes rain squalls would sweep in from the ocean, boiling
purple-gray clouds dragging heavy nets of rain that would
leave the town steaming afterward. Out on the flats I could see
boats and fishermen. I did not understand why my father had
left me again—even though it was Mother and I who had deserted him.

One day Daddy appeared, driving the Ford sedan, the one
he had bought in 1941 after coming home from the hospital.
He stayed a few days and then we all left, driving north, home-

ward. There was a palpable strain. Cousin Patsy came with us to spend a few months. She and I fought the entire way. I'm guessing, but given the severity of one incident, I think I was trying to punish my father.

One night we stayed in tourist cabins somewhere along Florida's east coast. Mother and Patsy slept in one cabin, Daddy and I in another. Daddy had bought me a model airplane, a wooden replica of a B–17, which he said we would build together when we got home. All day I played with the rough parts, and I continued to do so after supper at bedtime. I took the pieces out of the box and spread them around on the floor. There was a thick, elongated dowel that I knew would become the fuselage (even if I didn't know that word yet) and others that would be the wings, the engines, the tail.

Daddy told me to put them away and come to bed.

I continued to play.

"Son, put down the airplane and come to bed."

I studied the box. There was a painting of B–17s in action. In the foreground was one banking away so you could see the camouflage topsides and the sky-blue underbelly. Behind it there were other aircraft, including fighter planes, and bright orange pluffs of ack-ack. The gun turrets on the B–17s were spitting orange, too. That's what the little rods were for: machine guns.

"Son, put the goddamned plane down."

I refused.

The tug of wills intensified. I made the sounds of combat, swooping aircraft and sputtering machine guns. He jumped up from the bed, snatched the belt from his trousers, held me by the arm, and slashed at my legs. I screamed from terror and pain. Mother came from next door.

Later, I lay in the darkness on the bed with him. He began to pray.

"Oh, Lord . . . " he began.

"Oh, Lord," I repeated. He had always said my prayers with me.

"No, son," he said. "This is *my* prayer."

I don't recall the exact words beyond that moment, except it was a rambling plea for forgiveness, love, understanding.

I had nightmares. My worst fear was the death of my parents. The prospect of life without them was horrific. Nevertheless, I would not—could not—touch him.

The next morning, he and I went for a short walk along the beach near our cabin. He seemed meek, pale, and old in the pink morning light. I refused to hold his hand, but I told him that I would try not to fight with Patsy.

My only other memory of that trip was stopping at a monkey and parrot "jungle" near Savannah.

Neither of my parents ever spoke of the trip to Florida—or the incident that precipitated it—again.

6

At the end of that summer, Patsy returned to Key West, and our lives resumed familiar patterns. I entered the second grade, progressing rapidly with my reading. Mother had given me a set of *My Book House*, which I devoured. Daddy read to me the Grimm brothers' fairy tales and *Little Lord Fauntleroy*.

Many of the children who came to Lobeco Elementary were from deeply impoverished families. Some of the girls wore flour-sacking dresses; boys and girls alike shivered in cold weather from lack of proper clothing. Mother knew the school lunch was the one good meal they got a day. (Supper for them might be cornbread and cane syrup.) She let them go through the line as many times as they wanted. To me, the food was boring, institutional, the kinds of meals against which Mother railed. (Restaurants seldom satisfied her.) To many of those children, it was a godsend. Citrus fruits were a rarity, available only in winter. When the county sent out boxes of oranges or tangerines to supplement the lunch program, the children could be seen scrambling through the discards in the garbage heap, looking for one last exotic taste.

One raw evening that fall, I was playing with Little Harry at the store when my father came in. I rushed to meet him, as always. He was forever bringing me presents, notably comic books (which we called "funny books"). He was still dressed in his office suit and good shoes.

"You want to go fishing?"

I was a little startled, but thrilled.

"Yessir! Can Little Harry come, too?"

Harry, Sr., a small, sweet-natured man with a bald head and wire-rim glasses, smiled.

"I reckon Little Harry better stay here," he said.

We protested. But not too vociferously. Even then, I understood the import of it. I had been antic witness to my father's angling expeditions; but, save for the occasional cane-pole fishing, I had never taken part.

He took me by the hand and led me out into that gray and chill evening. We climbed into the Ford sedan and drove the short distance to the bridge. In the trunk (with its replacement mat), were his rods and a bait bucket. The rods he bought in those war years of scarcity were, by any standard, junk. They were made of cheap steel and were brittle. Once I accidentally shut the car door on one, and it snapped off like a crisp breadstick. My father stamped along the verge and cursed while I cowered against the seat in misery. The reels, however, were chromium- or nickel-plated Shakespeare level-wind bait casting models loaded with braided linen line.

I had that very much in mind when we got out of the car. He gave me a rod to carry and I took it like an acolyte accepting the Host.

"Watch your step, darlin'."

"Yessir."

We clambered down the sharp gray chunks of granite—trucked in from God knows what upland quarry. (There are no native rocks on the sea islands.) The wind drew a thick layer of clouds with it and cut through my knickers and woolen pullover. The tide was ebbing strongly, exposing the dark, slick rocks and the greasy mud along the marsh skirt.

"Perfect trout weather." Daddy grinned. He wasn't necessarily masochistic about fishing, but this was one of his favorite sayings. (In later years, I fished with a guide in Charleston named Jake Jones who was fond of saying, "Bluebird weather is for bluebirds.")

He had live shrimp in the galvanized pail, which was drilled through with multiple holes to allow free circulation of water and proper aeration for the shrimp, which die even faster than freshwater trout in oxygen-poor conditions.

"Now, listen, Bud," he said. "You've got to pay attention."

"Yessir."

The rods were rigged in what was then the prescribed way for speckled-trout fishing: the terminal rig consisted of a hook, a length of leader, a barrel swivel incorporated into a lead sinker, and—above that—a cork bobber that was free to run up the line until it reached a piece of rubber band twisted into it. This rubber band could be moved up and down to regulate the depth. He showed me how it worked. Then he hauled up the bait bucket and grabbed one of the shrimp, wet and kicking, in his fist. He threaded the hook carefully through the transparent carapace.

"Now I'm going to cast first and show you how."

He took the rod in his right hand.

"Put your thumb on the reel like this. . . ." He demonstrated. "You've got to thumb the reel, or you'll get a backlash. Understand?"

I probably didn't, but I probably also nodded assent. I was not about to admit ignorance.

"Now . . . you flip it out . . . ." He did so. The rig swung awkwardly, and the reel on the line spun too rapidly and knotted immediately.

"Goddamnsonofabitchin' . . ."

(Once, a few years later, when I used a swear word in front of my mother, she remonstrated swiftly. I retorted: "Have you ever heard your husband cuss when he gets a backlash?" She laughed so hard that she neglected to punish me.)

He snatched at the knots with quick, impatient fingers.

"Jesus H. Christ . . ."

He reeled in again and inspected the shrimp.

"Goddammit . . ."

He swung the rig again, and this time it landed with a

splash about ten yards from the rocks. The current was streaming out through the bridge abutments. The cork lay flat for a second or two, then came halfway toward upright.

"Damn it."

He reeled it in and adjusted the rubber band downward.

"The sinker was on the bottom," he explained. "You've got to keep it so the shrimp drags along just above the bottom; otherwise it won't look natural to the fish."

"Yessir."

On this cast, the cork immediately righted itself and begin to twist and bob in the swirling waters. He handed me the rod. He placed my hand in the correct position and put my thumb on the reel. The cork was laying flat again.

"Now, let a little line out . . ."

I lifted my thumb.

"That's all right, son, but when you do it, raise the rod tip a little. That lets out line and also makes the shrimp jump."

"Yessir."

"Now, you got to watch it carefully. Keep your eye on it. If it jumps up and down, or if it gets yanked under, strike!"

I did as I was told. I knew what he was talking about; I'd seen him do it dozens of times. My hands trembled. My whole body trembled.

I let the cork ride the tidal current until it was thirty or more yards away.

"Reel it in," Daddy said.

I cranked the rig in, and Daddy lifted it free of the water to inspect the shrimp again.

"Sometimes a crab'll chew on it and you don't know about it. Here . . ."

"Nossir. I want to do it."

He smiled a little and stood back while I swung the rig out again. I got a small backlash, which I insisted on picking out myself.

Finally, the cork began to float away along the marsh, exactly as it was supposed to do. Just below the mouth of a feeder creek, from which all the riches of the salt marsh were draining, the cork disappeared.

"Strike!" Daddy yelled.

I reared back on the rod and the line suddenly cut across the surface like a cheese wire, racing for the deeper water. I held onto the rod with both hands. Line streamed from the reel and burned my thumb. I didn't dare let up the pressure.

"Hold him! Hold him! Don't horse him! Let him run!" He hovered over me, his hands a frantic pantomime of what he would do—what I should do.

"Now reel . . . reel, reel! Don't ever give him slack . . ."

I did as he shouted. I held on. I reeled when he said "reel." I didn't try to force the fish toward me.

At last I managed to bring the trout in close to the riprap and Daddy, good brown cap-toe business shoes and all, skidded down the slippery granite chunks and grabbed the leader, swinging the trout up onto the rocks. He immediately seized it expertly right behind the head, folding down the dorsal fin, and removed the hook. He held it up. I was so excited, I dropped the rod.

"Jesus Christ, son, that thing cost money!"

I was nonplussed but couldn't have cared less. He brought the fish to me and hugged me. He took it higher on the riprap and laid it on a flat rock where it flopped and gasped, but it was too far from the water to escape. I moved up and sat just above it.

Daddy was grinning.

"Now Daddy's gonna catch one," he said.

I watched him out of the corner of my eye. My attention was focused on the fish. My fish. Fishermen's memories are notoriously suspect, even in the short term, but I think this one probably weighed about two pounds. Maybe a little less. Small potatoes by the standards of the Virginia Capes or Florida's Indian River, but it was a very respectable Lowcountry speckled trout. I sat and stared at it, not caring about the cold.

Daddy caught several more trout before the gloaming was subsumed by darkness and the tide had run out so much that the oyster shells at the mouth of the feeder creek were exposed. Daddy dumped out the last of his shrimp—they were dead by now, anyway, despite all efforts to sustain them. He put the trout in the bucket, and we drove back to the Wilsons' store. He bought me a Nehi grape and a package of parched peanuts—perhaps defiantly so, knowing that it would spoil my appetite and incur Mother's wrath. It was, after all, a man's rite, this celebration of the hunt.

I don't recall Mother's reaction, except that she probably feigned excitement. She probably also was thinking that, God help him, her only child was now infected with this disease.

I do know that in those precious few moments of hooking and playing my first speckled trout, my sporting preferences were fixed once and for all, the way my sexuality later was riveted in place by fifteen-year-old blonde cheerleaders in short skirts and bobby socks, and my taste in cars by a chance encounter with an MG-TD, BRG with leather bonnet straps, parked in front of Aimar's Pharmacy in Beaufort.

7

*S*o *began the* time when we were closest.

We were never absolutely attuned to each other—the way you can, or should, be with a spouse or a sibling, even a parent—but not me, not with my father. I hasten to append that he was in no kind mean-spirited, nor self-absorbed. Quite the opposite. He was demonstrative, but conservative; shy in the aw-shucks tradition of, say, a John Wayne character—and as emotionally translucent and easily read. It would be too glib to say we were just different and in some critical aspects doomed to disappoint one another. Perhaps we were too much alike—our magnets aligned like the little plastic Scotties. Nevertheless, we began to fish together. And I began to demonstrate a notorious propensity for luck. I have never claimed to be particularly adept, certainly not expert, at fishing. But lucky? Decidedly.

Whale Branch Bridge continued to be the locus of our efforts, affording, as it did, easy access to the marsh edge. The Branch was sufficiently narrow there that Daddy, at least, could cast out into the channel where the fish skulked during the colder periods. I trailed along whenever and wherever I could. He taught me to set a minnow trap, baiting it with several slices of stale bread and dropping it near the mouth of a culvert or in a deep spot in any little saltwater feeder creek. He taught me to conceal the line, too, covering it with bits of dried marsh grass. Once somebody stole one of his traps. His anger flourished for hours. He rated it as one of the lowest things one man could do to another.

Now and then, we would borrow a boat and he would row us to new fishing grounds. We caught trout and puppy drum in their feeding frenzies. We caught flounder in the channels, fishing minnows on the bottom. One day, when we were anchored just north of the Whale Branch Bridge, I hooked a small hammerhead shark that put up a ferocious tussle. It was by far the biggest thing I had caught to that point. Daddy whooped with delight. We also caught our share of catfish, and he taught me how to avoid their spines when dehooking them.

We soon discovered another vantage point from which to fish: the Seaboard Airline Railroad trestle over a tributary of the Branch.

The railroad was vital to Lobeco's raison d'être. The packing shed was on a short siding where the truck crops were washed, sorted, and loaded in freight cars bound for market. Since most of the trains that came through were headed by steam locomotives, there was a water tank, too. When an engine stopped for water, it was an object of great interest to everybody in the hamlet as it stood under the tower, chuffing, like an animal resting.

The Seaboard Airline Railroad also kept a telegraph office there, manned by Grady Byers Johnson's father. When there was a message for a passing train, Mr. Johnson had to walk a half-mile or more down the track and plant a small dynamite charge on the rails, a blasting cap detonated by the crushing wheels of the engine. The engineer then knew that he was to slow down, and the fireman leaned out of the cab and hooked his arm through a loop of string on a wooden hoop held aloft by Mr. Johnson, snatching the written instructions for the crew. On those extremely rare occasions when there was a passenger, Mr. Johnson went even farther down the track and stobbed magnesium flares into the ties, giving the crew ample time to stop.

In the summer, when Grady Byers was home, Mr. Johnson let us place the blasting caps. That is, Grady Byers, a teenager, was allowed to carry and place them. Little Harry and I tagged along and watched. And when we had done it, we retreated to the pine-scented woods and lay on our stomachs and watched and waited, the cap strapped to the shimmering rail like a blank-faced wristwatch. Long before the train appeared, we could hear its plaintive warning whistle. Cupping our hands over our eyes like binoculars, we strained to focus on the cap as the locomotive thundered into view. When the great wheels hit the cap, it exploded with a sharp report, and we leapt to our feet and cheered.

We also placed copper pennies on the rails. They were flattened into oblongs. We punched holes in the ends and strung them around our necks as "dog tags."

These tracks ran from horizon to horizon across the flat fields, bending just at the curvature of the earth to the north. The trestle was on the south side of the hamlet. From there the railroad slashed across island and hammock, through smoky junctions and grade crossings with names that appeared only on county road maps, all the way to the Savannah River and then Savannah itself. To the north, the right-of-way was a seldom-deterred gash in the primal Lowcountry forest until it reached North Charleston.

For Daddy and me, the trestle served a different purpose. Like the bridge, it offered access to fishing grounds unreachable except by boat. There was an inherent danger here, of course: that of being trapped out on the ties by an oncoming train. Daddy was cautious. He would check with Mr. Johnson, and then we picked our way out along the ties, carrying our rods and bait buckets. But one day we almost got caught.

Daddy must have lost track of time. The piercing shriek of the train's whistle sounded—and very near. The trestle began to tremble.

"Goddammit!" he shouted. "Run, son! Run!"

Without even bothering to reel in our rigs, we scrambled

toward the shore, paying out line as we ran until that came to the bitter end.

"Don't stumble! Watch your step!"

We made it to the Lobeco side and stood down on the grassy slope, sweaty, breathless, holding our rods in shaking hands, the corks and terminal rigs now dragged high into the marsh. The train went by slowly, the engineer and the fireman leaning out of the cab, waving, laughing. The engineer blew a double blast. He'd probably seen this a hundred times or more. Daddy and I were more careful after that.

8

The summer of 1945 was to prove momentous in many ways.

First of all, Daddy bought his first fly rod. It was split bamboo, of course. I kept it for many years and used it until the cane got so old it would remember the arc of its last backcast and became useless for fishing. But when it was new, it was a thing of righteous beauty and it further fulfilled the sporting need in him. He used it first in the rice fields along the Combahee River.

The Combahee (pronounced simply "Cum-bee") is an alluring body of water, part of an important watershed in the Lowcountry that also embraces the Edisto and Ashepoo (pronounced ED-is-toe and Ashy-poo, respectively) rivers in what is known as the ACE basin. All three eventually join the ocean in St. Helena Sound. The Combahee is formed by the confluence of the Salkehatchie and Little Salkehatchie rivers, which begin up where the sandhills begin to roll toward the feet of the Appalachian Mountains. It courses languidly through riverine forests before joining the diurnal push and shove of the tides. Most of the wetlands adjoining it are privately held, especially in old rice plantations.

One of these is Bonny Hall, owned by the Doubleday family of New York City, proprietors of the large publishing empire. From 1941 until the end of the war, Bonny Hall was the retreat of one of the Doubleday's most famous and valuable authors, W. Somerset Maugham. A special compound had been built to accommodate him. I recall it only vaguely, but Ted Morgan, in his biography of Maugham, describes it thus:

> ". . . [But] Maugham liked the house that Nelson [Doubleday] had built, which had three bedrooms, each with its own bath. It was white clapboard, with a fireplace wall paneled in Carolina pine. The bookshelves were filled with ready-made sets of 'great classics.' In addition, there were two cottages, one for his study and one for the servants, all black. There was Nora, the cook, Mary, the maid, and Sunday, the yardman, who wore dark glasses indoors because he thought it looked elegant. Sunday had a nephew called Religious, who did odd jobs around the place. The plantation overseer told Maugham, 'They're good niggers, they're humble.' The address was Parker's Ferry, Yemassee, South Carolina, but on his stationery Maugham crossed out the word 'Ferry' . . . "

(Irritatingly, Morgan does not explain why Mr. Maugham did this.)

All of it overlooked a boat landing (the old ferry landing?) where Daddy had secured permission to fish. As it happened, Mr. Maugham shared, along with the Attaways, the Johnsons, the Wilsons, the Chambers—and God only knows who else— a party telephone line. Every household had its own special ring. Ours was, I think, two longs and a short. But everybody knew everybody else's, and when the operator in Beaufort cranked Mr. Maugham's, the entire party line would pick up just after he did (discreetly, they thought) to listen to his queer British accent. (They also listened to each other.) Mother regarded him as rude and crusty.

I think I met him once. I think Daddy tried to sell him

a life insurance policy. I would give anything if I had even a recollection, much less a transcript, of such a conversation. But famous writers were of little consequence to me in those days, unless they fished. Mr. Maugham did not. Mother had met Ernest Hemingway while we were in Key West, and I was far more impressed with this when she told me he was a fisherman.

Nevertheless, under Mr. Maugham's dyspeptic stare and beneath a kind Carolina sky, we launched a canoe (belonging to whom, I don't know; Mr. McGill, the property manager, perhaps) and paddled out into the canals of the rice fields and along the Combahee banks. How Daddy acquired entrée to these private precincts I don't know either, except that he was well liked by most people and my parents had many friends in the Lowcountry's plantation society. It may have been given to be rid of his dolorous insurance policy sales pitches. (I heard him do this dozens of times and never understood a word he said, even when he sold me a policy. I think I, too, bought it just so he'd shut up.)

Rice cultivation in the Lowcountry ended generations ago, battered by storms and markets, but the old diked fields survive. Many were converted to duck-shooting ponds by the wealthy Yankees who bought up the plantations during the region's economic doldrums. Other fields were simply abandoned, and when the protective berms and floodgates began to disintegrate, they were laid open to the floods and tides and became important wildlife and fish sanctuaries. As we floated along the narrow, shallow waterways, the only sounds were the dip of our paddles and the softly rattling palings of the golden reeds. We were in the covert domain of red-winged blackbirds (rice birds), turtles, minks, and, of course, fish, notably largemouth bass and sunfish.

Daddy began to learn to use the fly rod. The fishing was so bountiful, it didn't matter how well or poorly he cast. He used little yellow popping plugs and sometimes, when a lazy backcast dropped the bug on the water behind him, a rapacious fish would gobble it up.

I used the bait-casting rod, tossing Hula Poppers and Hawaiian Wrigglers against the banks. Once I obviously made a too-slow and too-deep retrieve and caught the full attention of a mudfish, or bowfin. I'd never hooked a fish that fought as strongly—except the hammerhead shark. As soon as I brought it to the surface, I impulsively flopped it into the canoe.

"Great God, boy, no!" Daddy yelled.

Too late.

A few seconds later, we were both in the water (it was only about chest deep on me) watching as the bowfin, a nasty living fossil, snapped and chewed on everything it could sink its prehistoric teeth into, including the tackle box, aluminum thwarts, rope, and my smelly P.F. Flyers. Daddy finally beat it into submission with a paddle and we cautiously, tremblingly, got back into the canoe. The fly rod was fine. Daddy had held it above his head even as he scrambled out of the canoe.

"Goddamn, Bud, didn't you know that thing had teeth?"

"Nossir."

He laughed.

"That thing could have bitten off your toes!"

"Yessir."

It was the epitome of ugly.

Daddy make a great story of it that evening. And the mudfish joined the shark as part of our oral history.

9

Mother *shared none* of this. She, too, was a child of the steaming Lowcountry, but wanted no part of the marsh or the creek—except as provender. She had a deft and delicate touch with any food, especially seafood: speckled trout broiled with lemon butter or fried so that the outside was crisp but not greasy, and the firm white flesh flaked when you pierced the crust. Her deviled crab bore no resemblence to the dense, poorly seasoned, commercial versions where the crabmeat looks as if it has been forced through a food mill. Hers was light, filled with chunks of pure meat, and delicately spiced. She could, I swear by the memory of her blue eyes, cook a T-bone steak well done that was still juicy and tender. (Southerners have always preferred well-cooked meats. They didn't know what caused certain illnesses, but they understood that if you cooked your meat well done, there was less chance of it.)

She loved music and played the piano. Her favorites, she said, were classical. She played and hummed along, off-key—as painful as fingernails on a blackboard—and turned to her suffering audience with a smile. "I have perfect pitch," she would say. We never had the heart to contradict.

Daddy loved Tin Pan Alley.

But Mother was no snob. She dutifully, energetically pounded away on past favorites and current hits while Daddy accompanied her in his pleasant—if slightly flawed—baritone. They were both in demand at parties.

She also loved food and gardening. In this last, she took a Matissean view that a certain natural chaos was desirable. She let the Cherokee rose roam at will not only over its trellis, but up the drainpipe and along the gutter and the shutter. Her gardens tended to be less formal—although she admired the great formal European gardens for their artistry. Her taste ran to the English park with the pergola set just so ("... a length of colonnade / Invites us. Monument of ancient taste, / Now scorn'd but worthy of a better fate . . ."—Cowper), the hill and the copse modified to complement the bend in the river ("... a chief amusement of cultivated leisure," Nabokov wrote, regarding Jane Austen's *Mansfield Park*, in his "Lectures on Literature"), a little wilderness incorporated into the design. She loved fields of wildflowers, the fecundity of roadside verges, ditches filled with pussy willow.

"Crackers can't stand to see anything grow," she said. Often.

From a letter she wrote to me while I was a freshman in college:

> " . . . I miss you so very much. Sometimes riding to town, or home after work, I see things I wish you could see, too. Our countryside is particularly lovely this year due to the heavy late-summer rains. What we lack from the scope and panorama that hills give, we gain by lushness from the 'lowness' of the land. The feathery green grasses along the roadside are all interspersed with gorgeous wildflowers. Tall plumes of yellow goldenrod, purple spikes of fringed blue gentian, sassy little brown-eyed susans, usually pushing out in front in clumps (clannish of them!) and all softened by the misty, frothy white of the mallows and Queen Anne's lace filigreed through all like

the grace of gentle manners in an otherwise-cloying world. The scars of the woods fires of last spring are covered with the sporadic undergrowth and vines—everywhere vines! They look graceful and dainty from a distance, but being very parasitic to my camellias and azaleas (the little morning glories, especially), I have really whacked them with the swing cutter!"

Take that, Nature!

According to her birth certificate, she had been born in the little town of Hardeeville, but in fact it was the nearby community of Purrysburg (or Purrysburgh), settled by Swiss colonists under Jean Pierre Purry of Neuchatel, in 1732. The site was on the Great Yemassee Bluff, a narrow plateau lifting above the surrounding Savannah River Swamp, some 22 miles from the mouth of that river. For whatever reasons, the community never flourished, but remnants of it remained when Mother was a child. She became obssessed with it in later life, writing several papers on the settlement. In her notes for one such, she described a trip back there to visit the old cemetery (where, oddly, none of the family is buried):

"It was a partly cloudy day and we flitted in and out among the stones. The ground was a carpet of wild violets and leaves, the only sounds that of the birds singing in spring delirium. That area bordering on the National Wildlife Refuge as it does is a paradise for bird-watchers (also an Eden for snakes in hot weather). I like to think the mockingbirds were yodeling a requiem mass for the brave alpine souls who made a deep niche in our history and now rest in that lovely peaceful place. Along with Jean Ribaut and William Hilton, poor damned, doomed Jean Pierre Purry needs remembrance. The first two just came here and went away. Purry stayed and died for his illusion, his deception, or his ideal!"

Her father, Cholly Walker, had come here first as woodlands superintendant for the Hilton-Dodge Lumber Company in the early 1900s. The family later moved to Hardeeville as it grew and needed larger quarters. She wrote in a diary:

"This was home base for us for 14 years, summers in lovely Bluffton—but for all of us, Purrysburg was the enchanted place. Everything was here! Hunting, fishing, swimming, rowing the bateau up and down or across to Georgia. That wonderful river! We could splash in the shallows, make campfires on the banks, pick blackberries and plums, ride horses, of which there were many, all thru the woods in the timber-cart lanes and picnic forever and ever. What more could a child ask?"

A child, not much, perhaps; but as an adult, her sentiment shifted. She could no longer accommodate the heat and the humidity of Lowcountry summers.

"It's like the Black Hole of Calcutta," she would say, sitting on the screened porch, sipping iced tea, her skirt lifted to the oscillating electric fan.

But every evening she knelt in her flower bed, her milky, freckling skin protected by long-sleeved cotton dresses and a hat, a drop of perspiration clinging to the tip of her nose, her gloved hands digging busily, happily in the dirt. In later life, her features sagged into the fleshy countenance of England's Queen Mum, for whom she could have doubled. In her youth, she was quite beautiful. My cousin Pete Albrecht knew her at that age and says she was a heartbreaker.

But she did not fish. She hated beaches. Like the planter class that ruled the Lowcountry for centuries, she liked to go to the mountains in the summer. (She had attended Asheville Normal College for a while, in western North Carolina.) Even the foothills were more desirable than the swamps. There, the cool tramontane breezes blew away the aguish night air that left whole cities limp in its sultry grasp.

This was fine with my father. Especially now that he had his fly rod.

10

That summer—the summer I was eight—we spent a week in Hot Springs, North Carolina, a small town near the French Broad River, one of the better-known trout streams northwest of Asheville.

We stayed in a boardinghouse, a white-frame building set on a precipitous hillside. Our rooms were upstairs and opened onto a shaded porch with rocking chairs. Mother bought me a lined writing tablet, and I sprawled on the gray-painted boards and drew fantastic stories (stick men with otherwise-curiously-fat bodies) by the hour as she and Daddy rocked and read and sipped their bourbons and water in the evenings.

The town was noted for its steaming sulfurous and presumably curative waters, of which we partook, soaking in great concrete pools of it. We also walked a lot in the mornings. But the French Broad murmured its siren call to Daddy and we—he and I—fished it every day. He was eager to emulate the anglers he read about in the sporting magazines. He wanted to catch a trout—a real one—on a dry fly.

He had no boots or waders of any sort and simply took off his shoes and socks, rolled up his trouser legs, and waded out into the current, standing almost knee-deep in the swift, frothing waters, splashed now and then by unruly hydraulics, his thin white shanks braced against the onrush. I was relegated to the rhododendron-hung banks, given a cane pole and a can of earthworms. I watched him make the long, graceful sweeps of arm and rod, the heavy line pausing on the backcast, the loop of it catching the light and holding it, and then lashing forward, the tiny flies dropping delicately onto the river and racing, bouncing back toward him as he stripped in line.

One day we drove down to the river and found a stretch of it that appealed to him. He readied his fly rod, made sure I was properly equipped as well, and waded out into the stream. I threaded a worm on the hook and found a large, sunny flat rock in the near shallows. I sat on the leading edge of the rock and tossed my worm into the current, which snatched it and swept it around into the head of a large, protected pool. Almost instantly, a trout gobbled worm and hook. I yelled. Daddy almost went down several times as he stumbled over toward me. I flopped the trout onto the rock with as much grace as I'd shown the mudfish, but it was my trout, and by far the largest fish we took that week. To this day, I am unable to decide whether Daddy was prouder than mad, or vice versa.

This may have been the genesis of my perverse delight in occasionally fishing for trout with spinning gear (I do still fly-fish and enjoy it immensely). It is deadly. I once sat on a bank of the Beaverkill and watched a fly fisherman work a span of the river. When he had passed, I let the river rest for ten minutes and then cautiously began to work a Mepps around areas we both (the purist and I) knew trout were likely to be. In minutes, I had taken two fish. I glanced upstream in time to see him standing, glaring, at me. With great deliberation, he raised his fine R. L. Winston rod above his head and slammed it into the river—an action he instantly regretted and which horrified both of us.

On our way home from Hot Springs, we spent one night in Greenwood, South Carolina. The next morning, word flashed through the café, the hotel, and the town that the Japanese had surrendered. We tried to eat breakfast amidst the delirium and finally gave in, walking out into the streets to join the celebration. It was August 15, 1945.

11

A few weeks after the war ended, my father resigned from government service. A brief article in *The Beaufort Gazette,* quoted James M. Windham, Area Rent Director-Attorney for the Charleston Defense-Rental Area of the Office of Price Administration (only bureaucrats and presidents-for-life of Third World countries could come up with titles like that), who said: "We are very sorry to lose the services of Mr. Attaway, but he has elected to return to the operation of his insurance business, having advised all along that this would be his election when gasoline rationing permitted his securing sufficient gasoline to pursue this business . . . ." Et cetera, and a few nice words about his valuable services and contributions.

Read between the lines: he could now fish from Savannah to Charleston, from Beaufort to Orangeburg—and anywhere else he damned well pleased.

His resignation was effective on September 28, 1945. We moved to Beaufort.

The town lies on a point where Beaufort River folds itself around Port Royal Island, separating that from Lady's Island before widening suddenly into a false bay. On hot evenings, there always is a breeze that comes up the river from the ocean.

The island is low, rising to a brief crown overlooking the bay, and is mantled in crusty oak. Through this natural reredos, you can see the old white mansions with their red and green rooftops. Above all rise the whetted spires of St. Helena's Episcopal Church and the Baptist churches. The commercial district, where the bluff sweeps suddenly to near water level, looks deceptively busy. In summer, in the hard-edged, superheated Edward Hopper light, nothing moves at midday.

My parents bought a house on another sandy spike of the island called Pigeon Point. In those years, there was a total of five houses out toward the end of the point. Ours was a classical eighteenth-century sea island dwelling that sat some ten feet off the ground on brick pillars to lift it above storm surges, despite the fact that it was situated on a high bluff. A wide living room ran through the center. On the south side were two bedrooms and a bathroom (my parents' suite). On the north was a second bedroom (mine) with a bathroom, and the dining room. The kitchen was an appendage that jutted out of the back, clearly a modern afterthought. A screened porch ran across most of the front. The living room was paneled in native cypress, and the wainscoting in the dining room was cut from a single cypress log, three feet wide. There was no central heating, but every room had a fireplace. (To this day, I prefer a cool house and a cozy fire to central heating.) There were almost two acres of yard (which I would come to regret, as I was at the lawn-mowing age) and a wonderfully huge live oak in which I built a treehouse. Around the turn of the century, it had been used briefly as the county poor farm, the irony of which delighted Mother. She promptly had stationery printed with "De Po' House, Beaufort, S.C." as a return address.

Most important of all, the bluff on which it sat overlooked Brickyard Creek, which becomes Beaufort River around The Point (not to be confused with Pigeon Point). There was a wide expanse of marsh between us and the river, but a smaller, deep creek cut in close under the bluff. Today the creek has silted in and at low tide is a mud bank. In the late 1940s it never went dry and Carl Von Harten, who had a summer cottage next door, kept a cabin cruiser on a mooring there. A small cove came into the foot of the bluff on the left side of our property, affording a modest boat landing. Our nearest neighbors were the Kinghorns, who lived in a new house just the other side of the live oak.

When we took possession, the house was a shambles. It needed a new roof, it needed new siding, it needed new plumbing and wiring. The yard was knee-deep in broom sedge, and the bluff was a jungle over which you could not see from lawn level. It was just what Mother wanted: the ultimate landscaping challenge. She threw herself into it with passion and borrowed muscle—mine, my father's, hired men from the islands, sometimes trusties from the Beaufort County jail, who must have been desperate for money because they worked for a paltry wage, but who also must have been glad for the chance to get out of the jailhouse for a day. Rumor had it that there was a mass grave on the right front of the bluff where victims of the 1893 hurricane, South Carolina's Storm of the Century until Hugo in the late 1980s, had been buried. No amount of money could induce black laborers to go there. That part my father and I cleared ourselves. I have a scar on my left shin from a hatchet that ricocheted off a tough oak sapling.

There was one thing we hadn't counted on: the house was haunted.

A previous tenant laughingly told us about a poltergeist whom he called "Uncle." No one was sure whose ghost he was, but legend had it that there was a Yankee captain buried under the water oak just outside my bedroom window. Uncle was known to slam doors and jiggle crockery. We didn't think too much of the stories. They were easily explained away as capricious drafts in a very old house. But there were two incidents that defy explanation.

It was my custom (still is) to read in bed until I'm sleepy. One night I had just turned off the light and rolled over when I heard the door to my room open and footsteps came to my bedside.

"Momma?" I queried.

No response.

"Daddy?"

Still nothing.

I rolled back over and snapped on the light. There was nobody—or thing—there. Frightened, I ran across the house to my parents' bedroom. They were both asleep.

Some time after that, perhaps a year, I was home alone with my dog Winkie. We were in my father's room/office, and I was sitting on the floor, reading. Winkie startled me by beginning to growl. The hair on her back rose. I looked around. She was focused on the window on the south side of the house— which window, mind you, was some fifteen feet above ground level. Suddenly she began to bark furiously and back away from the window toward the door, terrified. We went outside and sat on the top step of the back porch, from which I could see lights in the Kinghorns' house. Winkie continued to growl off and on. I was too ashamed to go over to the Kinghorns', but too scared to go back into the room.

In due time, the yard was cleared, magnolia trees now defined the frontal offing, oleander flanked the steps, camellia and tea olive hemmed the foundation, and azaleas sprouted under the oaks. Truckloads of oyster shells were brought in to create a driveway.

At some point, Mother apparently thought to build a fence of sorts to demarcate our backyard boundary. To that end, several dozen cedar fence posts were deposited there one day. In my mind's eye, however, they were never meant as palings or posts. Clearly, they were the stuff of which rafts were made. (I was much under the influence of Mark Twain and— shortly thereafter—Charles Nordhoff and James Norman Hall.) One of my new friends in Beaufort was Poopy Mustard (now the Rev. Alan C. Mustard, Jr., an Episcopal minister). Poopy was a year older, but a kindred spirit. Poopy and I lashed a dozen of these posts together with two-by-fours and rigged a sail of an old bedspread. With an oar as a rudder, we launched our brilliant new craft and discovered quickly that square riggers do well off the wind, but do not point very high and are hell to row back against the tide. I think the raft finally was abandoned some way away from the cove. Mother was not pleased.

Perhaps it was this unfortunate introduction to the glories of sail that later made me a committed stink-potter.

12

The *refurbishing of* the house now more or less under control, Daddy turned his attention to the things that mattered most to him and me: the prospect of fishing.

He bought our first boat.

In retrospect, and in the unreliable, if felicitous, slag glow of memory, I recall that boat fondly. Like the boat Grady Byers Johnson and I had used at Lobeco, it was a flat-bottomed bateau made of cypress. It was fourteen feet long with stern and midships thwarts. Its chief virtue was that you could almost stand on the gunwales without tipping it. Even a low-powered outboard motor would send it rocketing over the water. But outboards were in the future. As a child, Daddy had rowed and sculled similar bateaux around Port Royal. He was determined that I would do the same. He bought a beautiful set of brass oarlocks and a set of oars. My education commenced.

I didn't mind at all. At first my oars dipped too deeply or skittered across the surface erratically. He sat in the stern and coached me—I wouldn't say patiently. Off the wind, or down-current, the bateau was quite fun to row. Otherwise, it was like trying to move a light cruiser. And God help you if it got stuck on a mud bank. The rich, gooey pluff mud, so revered for other reasons, sucked at the planking like a vacuum bag.

He also bought a castnet for shrimping, had it custom knitted on Lady's Island by one of the Gullah craftsmen there. It was three feet long—about perfect for the average person to use in the small creeks.

A castnet of this type is circular, with lead weights around its perimeter and drawstrings that lead through a central collar—traditionally carved from cow horn. These drawstrings are attached to a stout length of rope and pull the net closed.

We went out in the bateau the afternoon he brought the net home and rowed down toward the north end of our creek, where a sandbar jutted into the river. We anchored in the bight of the sandbar, and Daddy shook out the net. In the center of the boat was a No. 3 galvanized washtub.

"Now, darlin'," he began. "There's only one trick to this, really, and that's to remember to let go of the weights with your teeth."

A statement guaranteed to get your attention.

He demonstrated the throwing technique. First you shake out the net to ensure that the drawstrings are freed up and the rope is coiled and held in your left hand. After that, some of the top of the net is also gathered in your left hand. Then you reach down and lift one of the perimeter weights and hold it in your teeth. Finally, with your right hand, you reach around the skirt and grasp the net again. The throw is kind of like a golf swing: hips and shoulders rotate back to the left and then you swing to the right, leading with your right hand and swirling the net out. If done properly, the net spins slightly and lands with a big splash where you aimed it. This takes some modest amount of doing. If it is thrown improperly, the net will not open or open only partway, and any shrimp that might have been trapped under it escape easily. The whole idea is to approach an area where you have reason to believe shrimp are feeding and throw the net quickly and accurately. It sounds complicated, but in truth takes only a little practice to master.

As Daddy said, the only real trick is to remember to let go of the weight with your teeth.

Once I had mastered the essentials of the technique, we got out of the boat and waded over to the sandbar. A smaller, feeder creek came out of the marsh and we could see flickings on the surface of the water, indicating the presence of schools of shrimp. I approached cautiously—stalking, really—and swung the net back and forward. Not a bad cast. The net opened only about three-quarters of the way, but it sank rapidly beneath the surface.

"Now, darlin'," Daddy said excitedly. "Let it rest until you're sure it's on the bottom. All right . . . all right. Now, remember what I told you. Jerk the rope . . . thataboy . . . jerk it sharply to close it up quickly . . ."

I reached down and lifted the net. Water streamed away from it, but inside we could see a half-dozen or so good-sized white shrimp kicking, tangled in the mesh.

Daddy laughed and we splashed back to the boat to get the tub. The pleasure of seeing him so happy made me almost giddy. I was doing something to please him.

I don't think we caught an awful lot of shrimp on that first day, but I'm sure that whatever we caught, we ate. Like riding a bicycle, once you've learned to throw a castnet, you never forget how. Over the ensuing decades, I have spent countless—and sometimes fruitless—hours throwing a net from a boat; or, better still, wading up some sandy creek bed, in full and cautious pursuit. It's hard work. A forty-foot shrimp seine is a much more productive means of shrimping (a dip net baited with fishmeal balls and placed under a bright light at the end of a dock at night probably is best), but there is a great satisfaction in throwing a smaller net. Like fishing itself, some primordial need is consummated.

One evening, several years ago, we were cruising in the back bay of Virginia Beach, Virginia, aboard our twenty-foot outboard boat, *Tiburon*. It was about the middle of September, in a spate of perfect weather. We had been fishing off Cape Henry and had finally come in to relax, sip a glass of white wine, and remark idly on the homes along the pine-studded banks. Aboard that evening were my wife Robyn, her brother, Huntley Gill, and a friend, Carlos Merlo. In the starboard fishbox was a plastic pail and a castnet, which I use to catch bait. We began to notice long, undulating swirls just beneath the surface. Occasionally something wrecked the water's placidity. I eased the boat over, and we quickly realized that these were rivers of mullet come into the back bay to spawn. I turned the helm over to Huntley and stood in the bow with the castnet, bracing my legs against the rail, directing him left and right, feeling somewhat like Ahab pursuing a pod of whales. When we were close enough, I swirled out a cast and brought in a half-dozen mullet. I dumped them onto the deck where they slid, slapping frantically against the fiberglass, down into the cockpit, where they continued to flap and squirm. Carlos, an Argentine of Italian extraction, had never seen such largess. Amidst much laughter and occasional squeals, he and Robyn scooped up the mullet and dumped them into the fishbox.

(Carlos and I both love to cook and usually traded off culinary chores on our weekends at the beach. Although he speaks three other languages fluently, his English in those days was a little spotty. One Friday night, as we all assembled at the airport, I was carrying an insulated bag filled with fresh-cleaned soft-shelled crabs. Carlos immediately wanted to know what I was cooking ". . . for deener . . . ."

"Soft-shelled crabs," I said proudly.

He howled with laughter.

"No, no . . . seriously," he gasped.

"Soft-shelled crabs," I repeated, somewhat subdued.

He laughed again.

Later that evening, I sautéed the crabs and we all enjoyed them. It wasn't until the next morning that we discovered that Carlos thought I was saying we were going to have social crabs for dinner.)

For an hour, we continued the pursuit, until our fishboxes were filled. Daddy would have loved that, I thought. I can honestly say I have never been on the water is pursuit of some finny creature without thinking of him.

The bateau we had at Pigeon Point once had had a coat of some sort of dull red paint, which we never bothered to renew. This was a work boat in every sense, straightforward in design and concept (design is imprecise; nobody ever laid the lines for such a boat; it was built probably without the aid of any instrument more sophisticated than an educated eye), built to withstand harsh abuse. As such, it was also the perfect platform for crabbing. We always handlined for crabs, which makes it tantamount to sport. Each handline consists of about ten feet of stout cotton twine, one end of which is tied to a stick. At the other end, you tie on a chicken neck or back (or a fish head), and weight it with a small two- or three-ounce sinker. The bait is lowered into the water, and you wait for a crab to scuttle over and begin feeding. Crabs habitually do not sit in one place and chew, and it is this continuing motion that alerts you. You can feel it in the subtle tremors relayed to your fingertips, or you can see the angle of the twine begin to increase as the crab moves away. This is the sporting part: you then begin to bring in the handline, inch by inch, very slowly and very delicately, because crabs, feisty as they may be, are very skittish: almost every creature in the sea regards them as succulent. When the crab nears the surface, it becomes even more fidgety and escape-minded. Using a long-handled dip net, you scoop the crab up and drop it into the tub (or a bushel basket, an equally traditional means of transport). It's not as easy as it sounds. The dip net must be moved slowly under the crab, or it will drop the bait and swim away. And when you scoop, you have to do it very quickly. Many crabs are lost. As with shrimping with a castnet, there are more productive ways of catching a meal—like using wire-mesh traps (or pots, as they're called). But there is no sport in that. You might as well shoot your fish in the proverbial rain barrel—or buy your crabs at the fish market.

Taking turns rowing, Daddy and I ventured out from our own creek, going around Pigeon Point and up into another that paralleled the north side of the point and carried all the way back to a place called Horse Hole, where the creek ran close under a high bluff and created a grand arena for shrimping, fishing, or swimming. Sometimes, when Daddy was rowing, I slipped over the side and, holding onto the anchor rode, allowed myself to be towed.

Now I, too, was a creature of the sea, my senses greatly heightened as the water sluiced around me. The only sound was the creak of the oarlocks and the casual susurrus of the oar blades dipping. The creek burbled along the edge of its banks. The mud, exposed in the dropping tide, popped in the heat. Now and then, shrimp showered across the face of a shallow feeder creek with a sound like a handful of birdshot being thrown into the water. Above, the sky was bright and empty, a few fat clouds hanging onto the landmass to the west, portending possible thundershowers later.

The boat yawed around a point of marsh, sideslipping in the current. A startled great blue heron flapped away with an ear-shattering croak. Daddy began to sing:

"I got a home in de rock, don't you see?
I got a home in de rock, don't you see?
Just between de eart' and sky,
Where my poor Jesus bled and die,
I got a home in dat rock, don't you see?"

Keeping away from the barnacles on the bottom, I dipped beneath the surface. The creek smelled of fish and salt and the water seemed thick and clinging, unlike the tepid, thin bathwater of my evening tub. It made my skin tingle. I never minded the quick, unexpected pricklings when shrimp and small fish ricocheted off my limbs or torso. There were sudden unexplained noises, the splashes of predator and prey. The marsh itself seemed to sing to me, almost as if I were hearing the ringing emptiness of Lobeco; only this was alive and vibrant, a muted, aphonic chorus of rustling leaves, of creatures unseen slithering across the shiny surface, of the faint clacking and bubblings of china-back fiddler crabs waving their claws territorially, of the mud itself drying and crazing into jigsaw patterns. There would be bird cries, too, sometimes quite near and raucous, like the giant blue heron; but more often, faint and plaintive, the sweet shrill of red-winged blackbirds, the *cank-cank-cank* of marsh hens, the flittering twits of sparrows, and the distant, echoing caw of a crow. Under the surface, you could hear the pinging, clicking escape of shrimp. Where the boat disturbed the water's surface, the creek lapped against the shore in fine, rebounding wavelets that seemed to imitate the slap-slap of the flat hull on the tide, and the light, so pure and crisp in its mirror image of the sky, was shattered into Magellanic Clouds of intense reflection.

Sometimes we rowed for the pure pleasure of being out on the water. In the fall, however, when the water began to cool down and the trout came back up from the deep holes where they had languished, we fished. We fished around the mouths of the creeks, and now and then we would row arduously across Brickyard Creek to Factory Creek and float our baits in the lee of the oyster factory. In the late 40s, osytering was still done commercially from sailing craft (much as it still is in some parts of the Chesapeake Bay), the oyster boats coming in on the tide, their orange, gaff-rigged sails tight in the evening breeze. Brickyard Creek (and Beaufort River) was part of the Intracoastal Waterway and rife with all sorts of watercraft: local shrimp boats, sleek cabin cruisers downbound in winter (the "snowbirds") or returning in spring, small boats such as ours, and long tows of barges, their freeboard all but exhausted under hogsheads of tobacco.

The creek, the river, and the marshes fronting our house were alive with seabirds: herring gulls, laughing gulls, and ring-billed gulls wheeled around the shrimp boats; least and royal terns hovered and dove; willets, plovers and ruddy turnstones, godwits, sandpipers, egrets and herons tiptoed along the edge of the tide; oystercatchers and black skimmers swooped across the shallows. No other sound in the world so defines a milieu as the wild cries of these creatures. I built a blind behind a deadfall of an old live oak and spent hours there watching, listening, and compiling the beginnings of my life list.

13

N ow *that we* had the boat, which we kept anchored in the cove, I began to provide for the family table (on a somewhat sporadic basis, but occasionally I got lucky with net or handline), and—most important—it was entrée to all the creeks and rivers around Beaufort.

Poopy Mustard was as happy to see the boat as I. We both loved scouting. I was a stalwart member of the Flaming Arrow Patrol, Troop 1, Coastal Carolina Council, BSA. I loved camping. So did Poopy. When we weren't off on an official camping trip with the scouts, we did it on our own, often in the company of his younger brothers, Billy and Charles. We rowed the bateau over to Goat Island for a night or a weekend.

Goat Island is now privately owned and is somebody's near-perfect home, but then it was the ideal playground for twentieth-century Huck Finns and Tom Sawyers. The island was more or less half-moon shaped, dense with pine, oak, and palmetto. A high bluff hung over a deep creek and a narrow, sandy beach. Somewhere in its center were earthen rings, no doubt left by charcoal makers; but, in our imaginings, they were Indian mounds where cabalistic rites had been performed, perhaps the site of horrible human sacrifice such as the ones depicted by LeMoyne in his sixteenth-century engravings of life on the islands. (Similarly imaginative boys today probably ascribe them to aliens from outer space; flying saucers had not yet come into vogue.)

Daddy had given me a two-man tent for my birthday, a war surplus U.S. Army mountain/jungle model, green on one side, white on the other (and completely reversible). It had a floor sewn in and vents at either end. Mosquito netting over the door and the vents made it perfect for use in our subtropical jungles.

On Goat Island we caught crabs, fish, and shrimp and cooked them over a campfire. We were anything our imaginations wanted us to be, from the Swiss Family Robinson to U.S. Marines. Now and then some of the older boys (notably Stanley Bond, whose brother Henry "Goat" Bond sometimes joined us) would surreptitiously row over and fire shotguns and make strange noises to scare us. In truth, we always hoped they would. It was part of the mystique of camping. Lowcountry ghost stories and legends also filled our fantasies, especially the headless Huguenot, René Rondolier, roaming the forests, looking for his hydrocephalic skull.

Beaufort itself was a nearly perfect small town in which to grow up—if you were white. (One must be honest.) The population then was less than 5,000. Bay Street was paved with bricks, and many of the side streets were sand, with purple phosphate showing through in places, or were of crushed oystershell, like our driveway. Pigeon Point Road, in fact, was paved only partway to our house—for about a thousand yards, after branching off from Boundary Street. Along this part there were a number of houses and a small project built during the war for married marines. About halfway out, however, the paving ceased. You passed between two tabby pillars, and it was dirt from then on. No sidewalk. I especially remember one night when I was about ten. I had to ride my bicycle home from the movies. There were two theaters in town: The Breeze, on Bay Street, and The Palm, on Boundary. Both were owned by the brothers Smith, but The Palm was open only on Friday and Saturday nights and showed either cowboy pictures or horror films. On that particular night, I had gone to see *Frankenstein* for the first time. And then I had to ride down this dirt road by moonlight. The friendly, framing live oaks were, of course, transformed into something out of *Snow White and the Seven Dwarves*, every branch a hideous claw snatching at me. Boris Karloff lumbered through the insidious shadows, hands outstretched to rip apart my pitiful bones if I stumbled.

Within a few years, the postwar boom swept over Beaufort, and houses began to sprout all over Pigeon Point where previously only sassafras and saw palmetto had grown. For about three years, though, the woods were wild and wonderful. We fished and crabbed in the creeks, hunted squirrels and rabbits, swung Tarzan-like from the lianas, and camped. Today my idea of roughing it is doing without room service, but as a youngster I would rather sleep outside in my tent than anywhere—and did so. The tent was almost a permanent installation under the big live oak. When I had a friend over for the night, we usually slept outside.

The town, particularly The Point, was filled with old houses, tangled gardens, and shady greens. Unlike Charleston, where many of the houses are built sideways to the street and crowded together, Beaufort's architecture consists in the main of plantation houses brought to town and surrounded by large fenced yards. It was—and is—a place of unimaginable charm and beauty. In the company of Poopy Mustard, Rivers Varn, Jr., Arthur Marscher, Jr., John Mark Verdier, Michael Cory, and DuPre (Pree) Jones, I managed to get into boyish devilment— of a benign variety, like swiping green pears from Mrs. Helen Christiansen (one of God's wonderful people; she was the librarian at Beaufort Elementary), or soaping automobile windshields on Halloween. Pree's father was a doctor, and the family lived in a huge old house on the corner of Bay and Carteret streets, right at the foot of the Lady's Island Bridge. From its high piazzas, we would launch the occasional water balloon at unsuspecting pedestrians. For which we were duly punished.

Bratty, yes, but not juvenile delinquents. Much of our energy was spent in the creeks and marshes. Crabbing was a favorite activity. We did this from our bateau and from docks. And we swam. Every day, from the first of May until the end of September, we (at least I) went swimming somewhere. We bogged across mud flats in our bare feet and inevitably sliced a toe on an oyster shell. We skinned our shins climbing trees. We used the tabby ruins of an old house as a fort. We raced bicycles and trudged across town with our roller skates to the only hill with a sidewalk, a one-block stretch of Craven Street. Billy Marscher, Arthur's older brother, made a vehicle consisting of a few boards on an old baby carriage frame, and with this we went careening down the high bluff on Bay Street, willfully and gleefully crash-landing in the edge of the marsh. On particularly favored weekends, some set of parents or other would drive a car load of us out to the beach at Hunting Island or to Burckmyer Beach, right down the river. Hunting Island was preferred because it was a barrier island and we could frolic in the long, lazy Atlantic combers. Burckmyer Beach was less attractive, having no surf, but the Marine Corps had used it to practice amphibious landings, and the remains of several vehicles were still awash. (Hunting Island had been used as a gunnery range and for years after the war, quantities of unspent .50 caliber machinegun rounds would surface in the sands. I even found a practice bomb there, and it became part of my boyhood bedroom decorations—along with pennants and the usual paraphernalia.)

Crime in Beaufort was virtually nonexistent. There was only one policeman, Artie Heape, whose "office" was a telephone-booth-sized structure attached to the side of Wallace & Danner department store, where a short side street sloped suddenly down to the Beaufort Yacht Club—a glorious title for an organization best known for the gin-rummy games played on its wide screened porch. I learned early on that Daddy played there every Wednesday afternoon. If I hung out at his elbow he would—sooner than later, to be rid of me—give me a quarter, which would get me into the movies, buy me a bag of popcorn, and leave a penny for a sucker.

Nobody locked their front doors. Nobody took the keys from their automobile ignitions. About the only crime was the occasional brawl when marines and teenaged town boys clashed over the favors of a young lady at the weekly Friday night square dances at the Community Club.

The big events of every summer were the sailboat races sponsored by the South Atlantic Yacht Racing Association. The races moved up and down the coast, from town to town, in what now seems an astonishingly cavalier attitude toward work. How, one wonders in retrospect, did these people earn a living? The races lasted four days, Thursday through Sunday, but the partying began on Wednesday night, when all the racers came to town. In Beaufort there were street dances by the bandshell in front of the courthouse. And on any given night, there was much beer drinking and shagging at the Yacht Club. (When the movie *Shag* came out a few years ago, it was reviewed in *The New York Times* and the *Wall Street Journal*, both of whose critics referred to shagging as ". . . apparently a minor dance craze in South Carolina in the 50s and 60s." Or words to that effect. I wrote a rebuttal, pointing out, among other things, that the shag is, by act of the state legislature, the official dance of the Palmetto State. It ran on the Op-Ed page of the *Times* and elicited extraordinary response from South Carolinians and expatriate South Carolinians all over the country.)

The popular boats in those days were Moths, Snipes, Lightnings, and an array of one-designs and inland-lakes scows. The biggest of the fleet were the Sea Island One Designs, which class had, to my knowledge, only three boats. They were huge flat-bottomed scows. Beaufort's entry was *The Syndicate*. When it won the cup one year, Artie Heape emptied the magazine of his .45 pistol. (He fired a single shot in the air to signal a winner anyway.) I crewed occasionally on some of the boats. One of my uncles even offered to buy me a Moth (the most popular class) if I crewed all summer. But sailing was never to become central in my life. I was a fisherman. Even though I was the editor in chief of *Yachting* magazine for more than two years, "sailboat race" remains one of my favorite oxymorons. (America's Cup racing notwithstanding. The America's Cup series off Freemantle in 1987, which I attended on behalf of *Yachting,* was quite extraordinary. Yacht racing on the Beaufort River, however, often was a drifting contest under slatting sails.)

As noted earlier, much of Beaufort County was isolated from the rest of the world. The Lady's Island Bridge, for example, dated only from 1926. Hilton Head wasn't connected to the mainland until the late 1950s. Some of the other islands remained out of the commercial and cultural loop until the 1960s. Beaufort's second bridge, across Broad River, which cut the driving time to Savannah in half, also dates from the late 1950s. If there was any salutary effect of this, it was to preserve almost intact the Gullah culture. The immediate and practical consequence on my youth was that I knew the islands, a world unto themselves, before the onslaught of tourism brought golf courses to replace the native savannas and the dreaded condos obtruded over pine and palmetto. The Varns, for example, had a cottage on Eddings Point, which seemed so remote. It is now a densely packed suburb on St. Helena Island. As children, we found arrowheads at the foot of the bluff there and tried to run a crabbing business one summer.

One of the more memorable characters in Beaufort's recent history was its longtime sheriff, J. E. ("Ed") McTeer. Descended from some of the county's most notable families, Sheriff McTeer, the "High Sheriff of the Lowcountry," ran that department for more than forty years. In so doing, he tramped almost every square foot of every inhabited island and many that were not. He not only spoke Gullah fluently, his law-enforcement duties compelled him to master the arcane intricacies of obeah, or black magic. He became the only white witch doctor in America. He was a tall, lanky man with courtly manners. The McTeer family lived in a big house on Bay Street, overlooking the bluff. Behind this was a smaller dwelling that he had converted into a personal museum containing many arrowheads, pottery, and bottles from the Colonial period, and even a small brass cannon he dug from the sands of Bay Point.

In the late 1940s, Beaufort had no radio station (that and television were five or more years away), and *The Beaufort Gazette,* Howard P. Cooper, editor and publisher, was the medium and the message. On election nights, the townspeople gathered around the front of the *Gazette* offices on Charles Street. As results were telephoned in (or radioed by Ed McTeer's deputies, in some instances), Howard Cooper posted them on a huge blackboard propped against the building. Barrel Landing, with two registered voters, was always the first precinct reporting. It was sort of like Maine in national elections: as Barrel Landing went, so went the county. They were all Democrats in those days, and the winner of the Democratic primary was a shoo-in on election night. That these selfsame people are now steadfast Republicans, by and large, is one of the great political metamorphases of the century. The party of Lincoln in *Beaufort?* Keep in mind, when I was in junior high and high school, the system was segregated, and the United Daughters of the Confederacy was a potent organization. We didn't celebrate Lincoln's birthday, we sat in assembly on Jefferson Davis's birthday and listened to little old ladies extol with mephitic breath the recent (oh, so, in the minds of many) demise of the Confederacy. There is a large National Cemetery in Beaufort, holding the dead of both sides from the War Between the States, but we did not celebrate Memorial Day, either. That was known locally as Decoration Day, and the blacks would come to town for a weekend-long party that featured a parade and a traveling carnival. They set up food stalls along Boundary Street near the National Cemetery, and it was they who decorated the graves of the Union soldiers and sailors buried there.

July fourth was honored, of course. After all, three signers of the Declaration of Independence were from the Lowcountry.

14

Among those settling and readjusting in the aftermath of the war were my Aunt Helen and Uncle Boots Albrecht. Boots (his real name was Charles Beaufort) had spent several years stationed in Boston with the U.S. Navy, and returned to found a logging business in Charleston and Georgetown counties. They built a house on the back side of Sullivan's Island and eventually Aunt Helen's son, my cousin Fleetwood (aka Pete), who had served in U.S. Army Intelligence in China during the war and then taken a degree in forestry from Louisiana State University, joined the family business. This was vital to my well-being because, as I approached adolescence, the inevitable collision with my parents, fueled by rebellion (a teenager's sworn duty to annoy all adults, especially parents) and raging hormones, began to tear at the fabric of our small family unit. As so often happens, I found it easier to talk to almost any adult other than my parents and Aunt Helen became my confessor and chief supporter. The timing was perfect, because Pete was now grown and I became a surrogate son. (When Pete was at the same stage in his life, it was my mother who became his best friend.

"No two people on earth were ever so attuned to each other as Claire and I," he remarked recently.) So I began to spend weeks at a time during the summer on Sullivan's Island.

Unlike my mother, Aunt Helen loved the water and the marshes. She adored crabbing and fishing. Uncle Boots bought a sixteen-foot Halsey, a local product, and powered it with a 25hp Johnson outboard, then about the biggest motor around. We fished up and down the Cooper and Wando rivers, and even ventured offshore—a brave thing in so small a boat. Actually, it was less foolhardy than it sounds. Charleston Harbor is protected by massive jetties that go well out into the Atlantic. Here, beyond the mouth of these jumbled chunks of granite, the land slipped behind the earth's curvature, and even the lighthouse on Sullivan's Island occasionally was snuffed by the swell. The ocean here was clean, free of the riverine sediments that turn even the surf brownish, and rapacious schools of Spanish mackerel and bonito slash through the seas. I have a photograph of Aunt Helen and me with twenty-three Spanish mackerel spread out at our feet in the carport of their home.

There also were several times each year when the Attaway household on Pigeon Point was invaded by cousins, uncles, aunts, friends, and friends-of-friends, notably when the speckled trout moved up into the creeks in fall and spring, and word would be flashed from one end of the state to another. Most people's associations with the autumnal equinox usually gyrate around the tesselations of color that transform the woodlands, the sudden appearance of apples and apple cider in the market, perhaps the pungency of wood smoke hanging on a cold and still evening. Mine embrace recollections of oyster roasts and bourbon-bruised voices singing late into the night to my mother's piano accompaniment—followed by the sonorous thunder of guests asleep all over the house, even on cots in the living room. The next morning, we'd all be standing along some marsh fringe, or sitting, freezing, in our boat, floating live shrimp for specks.

In late spring, as the trout and puppy drum begin to move back into the creeks, the larger drum—channel bass, we called them—(they are known almost universally elsewhere as redfish) cleave the marine alps off the beaches and the ponderous blackdrum begin to appear in the sounds. There was an old saying in Beaufort: "When the gnats bite, the drumfish do, too." The blackdrum were caught in deeper water and usually on handlines. One day, as I walked down Bay Street, I saw "Toots" Martin, a barber and a very large man who always reminded me of Jackie Gleason in his bartender role, bending over long loops of twine stretched out along the sidewalk. I asked him what he was doing.

"Treatin' my line with ass-a-fetidy," he said matter-of-factly. It was his opinion that using asafetida somehow attracted fish. (I've never tested the theory, but Mr. Martin was quite famous for catching very large drumfish.)

That fishery never appealed to Daddy. But the red drum, or channel bass, in the surf, had the same effect on him as the Lorelei on German sailors. Off to Hunting Island we went.

Before the state park was fully developed (and desegregated) the north end of the island was reserved for blacks, the center for whites, and the south end was left alone. You could walk to that deserted extremity along the beach, or you could take the one road maintained by the resident forester. The road, like water, followed the path of least resistance as it wound through the virgin pine and saw palmetto, two white ruts of purest beach sand—and treacherous. This was where Daddy also taught me how to drive on sand and how to dig myself out of it. Usually it was worth the effort, because the south end of the island was a fragment of paradisaical Lowcountry. Even though the southern ends of these barrier islands are where the sands accrete, the south beach at Hunting Island had washed severely in storm tides. Great live oaks had toppled, and the rising waters would race and foam around the barnacled limbs. Crabs and small fish sought shelter in and around these encrusted trees, and this, of course, attracted the bass.

We had no proper surf-fishing gear. We used the same bait-casting rods and reels we used for trout. For bait, we used cut mullet or live crabs that we found trapped in the tidal pools at low tide. Casting a four- or six-ounce sinker with a slab of mullet is not easy with that kind of gear, but a hookup was electrifying. Many was the time we got a strike and then were forced to race along the beach, keeping pace with the charging fish. We lost more than we caught. Later, in the early 1950s, Daddy and I did much of this kind of fishing in the company of a new near-neighbor, Jim Till, who exerted some considerable influence over my developing sensibilities. Jimmy was a handsome, articulate young man, then studying for a foreign-service career at the University of Virginia. He loved golf and fishing. He never went into the diplomatic service, but had a brilliant career at the *National Geographic* magazine, becoming its youngest-ever advertising director. Twenty-five years later, when we were both divorced and at loose ends, he graciously let me share his apartment on New York's West Side for a spell. On hot summer evenings we sat on the balcony overlooking 71st Street and sipped wine and talked of those warm summer days at Hunting Island. He remembered my father fondly and well.

15

t didn't take long for the postwar boom to hit even isolated Beaufort. Despite the drastic cutback in the military presence (the Naval Air Station was shut down, but a new Naval Hospital eventually was built, and Parris Island kept on training recruits for the Marine Corps), there was a surge in population and the economy. For the first time, and—in retrospect, perhaps the only time—my father's business blossomed. He sold a $100,000 whole-life insurance policy to John M. Trask, Sr., and the commission from it propelled him in the New York Life Insurance Company's Top Club. He had been invited to regional sales meetings and conventions before, but this was his first invitation to The Big Dance, as they say. The following summer, Daddy and Mother took off on a trip to Canada, to Québec (which we pronounced Kwee-beck), where the insurance company was holding its Top Club meeting at the Chateau Frontenac. They drove up along the Atlantic Seaboard and even toured a bit of southern Québec before moving into Québec City itself. For two people who had known nothing but the South (although Daddy had spent some time in New York City when he was in the navy), it was astonishingly foreign. The Québecois are noted for their gargling, unintelligible interpretation of the French language, which made it all the more alien, all the more alluring—especially to Mother.

My father had earned a reputation as a storyteller—of Gullah tales, that is. There were several other white men, notably Gary Black of Beaufort and Dick Reeves of Charleston (both of whom either wrote books or made tape recordings) who were more famous, but Daddy nonetheless was much in demand at functions (all white and usually all male). These tales were stories in which the Gullah-speaking black people were seen as quaint (at best), stupid sometimes, or—more often than not—simply inept with Standard English. They were stories in the dinner-plate eyes, shuffling feet, Stepin Fetchit mode. Some of the humor was quite gentle, unless you happened to be black, because the black man always was the butt. Today it is unthinkable. (I listened recently to a tape Dick Reeves made in the 1960s and it is apalling, now, to think that these things continued as long as they did.) It is indefensible, but explainable given the tenor of the times; Hollywood led the way with the stereotype, an outgrowth of minstrel shows.

Daddy had told his Gullah stories many times at luncheons in the Savannah or Charleston branch offices, through which he worked. His pals there touted him to the convention committee, which decided to add his "act" to the entertainment at dinner one evening. He dressed in a long black frock coat and affected a cane, his interpretation of an old black minister. (I have a photograph of him on the stage at the Chateau Frontenac.) He told his stories. Somebody from the Savannah or Charleston offices may have tittered; Mother surely smiled (she'd heard them all many times before), but other than that, there was a silence interrupted only by the chink of china and the tinkle of silverware. In the days of vaudeville, they would have hooked him into the wings. He was utterly humiliated.

And, as if that weren't enough, when it came time for dessert, Daddy—who at this point had had it with all things foreign and unfamiliar, especially the French language and menus that listed things he not only didn't know how to pronounce, but couldn't imagine people would eat—decided that he wanted some ice cream.

"Vah-kneel-ah?" the polite little waiter asked in his heavily accented English.

"No, goddammit!" Daddy erupted. "Just plain ice cream."

Despite these contretemps, he was convinced that he had been "abroad"; culturally, he was a whole man. (He never again even contemplated leaving the Lowcountry, much less the United States of America. Mother, on the other hand, spent the last five or six years of her life flying all over Europe and the British Isles and loving it.)

16

Emboldened by his travels, enriched (so to speak) by a growing business, Daddy eventually tired of dealing with the old bateau and bought a Thompson runabout, a handsome little boat with varnished thwarts, a round, almost canoe, hull with a modest tumblehome, and (God does listen to prayer!) an outboard motor. The motor was only a 7.5hp Firestone, but the Thompson's flat aftersections made the boat jump out of its hole and skim the tides like a mullet with a tarpon on its tail. The boat would fly. Further, he had purchased a trailer.

Now we really began to fish.

Where before we had to be content to walk along the banks of the Combahee or the Ashepoo, or paddle a borrowed canoe into the rice fields, we could trailer our new boat to any landing and ply waters only dreamed about.

Early every spring, the anadromous shad swarm up the Combahee in a spawning frenzy, much as they do in virtually every clean freshwater river on the eastern littoral. Daddy had always wanted to explore this fishery more completely, and now we did. Dropping the boat in at the landing on Old U.S.

17, near Yemassee, we trolled our silver spoons upriver and down and back again, in leisurely pursuit of the bony but delicious herringlike fish. The river in this stretch is wild, primeval (the Amazon, the Nile, or the Congo, in my boyish imagination), where in hot weather you do not dare let your boat slide under overhanging tree limbs because snakes might loll there, hunting frogs and insects. I was Stanley in search of Livingstone, together we were Martin and Osa Johnson (no specific roles assigned). I eyed the riverbank for crocodiles. (Alligators were common.) A thicket of wild cane held painted warriors with poisoned darts.

"Son—goddammit, watch your line!"

I was snagged again on a sunken tree limb.

There are two varieties of shad, the American and the hickory, both of which ascend the rivers of the Lowcountry. The American shad (*Alosa sapidissima*) is considered the more desirable of the two. The hickory (*Alosa mediocris*—an unfortunate appellation to bear for all eternity) is more prevalent in southern waters, but, according to Al McClane's *Standard Fishing Encyclopedia*, the Combahee is one of the primary streams for the American variety. I could not begin to tell you which we caught, but suspect it may have been both. The hickory, apparently, likes the smaller feeder tributaries—places we now were free to explore. Whatever, whichever, we caught, Mother broiled the flesh and sautéed the roe in bacon fat and that, for your edification, served with steaming hominy is something that may safely be placed under the delicate nostrils of the most fastidious potentate.

In 1941 dams were completed across the Santee and Cooper rivers, creating Lakes Moultrie and Marion, taming hitherto unmanageable waters, and trapping a large, spawning colony of striped bass—with spectacular and fortunate consequences for anglers. The success of this fishery has been imitated in many places throughout the United States. Daddy and I tried it on our own several times, trailering the Thompson up to the landings and threading our way through the drowned forests with very limited success. More than a decade later, when I worked on the newspapers in Charleston, I fished it with local guides and caught a fair share. But I do remember being put off on a sandbar to relieve myself and realizing that I was standing in a trove of Indian artifacts, mostly pottery shards. (I think I was Roy Chapman Andrews at this point; the shards weren't dinosaur eggs, but fired my imagination none-theless.) Daddy was less than sanguine about this interruption of our fishing.

Even if our luck on the Santee-Cooper lakes was nil, we caught the occasional striper (called rockfish here) while troll-ing the Combahee. In no literature on the subject that I can find is there any mention of why these bass, which are anadro-mous, like the shad, are not taken in the surf, as they are in New England. They are caught only when they head up the rivers.

17

These youthful fancies of mine may have been the germinating bud of the problems that would beset our relationship in coming years. I read Hemingway and dreamed of Africa. Daddy read periodicals and dreamed of my becoming a professional baseball player. His sporting heroes were Ty Cobb and Babe Ruth. If I had any sports heroes at all, it pretty much could be narrowed down to one: Ben Hogan. We almost came together on this, because he would talk at length of the great Bobby Jones. But he no longer played the game. I never understood this. I never will. I guess I failed to ask him. My parents never joined the country club; so, in order to play golf I was reliant on the kindness of friends whose parents did belong, notably Steve Schein, whose father owned Beaufort's largest department store and who later became a classmate at the University of North Carolina.

I suppose they did not join because they never really had the money. (That one great year when he made the Top Club was to be the apex of his sales career.) I do remember broaching the subject on occasion and being rebuffed with an angry shake of his newspaper and a muttered deprecation or two into his bourbon. I think he was just embarrassed.

Aunt Helen, herself a keen golfer in her youth, gave me her old clubs. They were wooden shafted, the leather grips were worn smooth, and they had no numbers, but names, like baffy and spoon and cleek. With these and balls retrieved from the water hazards at the Lady's Island Country Club, I spent hours on our front lawn (nearly two acres, mind you) working with the short irons, chipping to a peach basket. To this day, I am short and erratic off the tee, but reasonably accurate around the green.

This did not please Daddy, nor appease him. One day, he came home and into the living room where I was, typically, sprawled on the rug, reading. He had something behind his back and that look of expectancy on his face that told me he had brought a present. I leapt up.

"It's not even your birthday," he said. He grinned. He produced a bat, a baseball, and a glove. He (notoriously pinch-penny in some ways) had spared no expense. A real Louisville Slugger, and a Wilson fielder's glove.

I took the glove and slipped it onto my hand.

"What a mitt!" I said. Or words to that effect. I meant only to convey enthusiasm, for his benefit.

His face fell.

"It's not a mitt," he said, as if I had just called a piece of the True Cross a railroad tie, "it's a glove. Catchers use mitts. First basemen use mitts. This is a glove, a fielder's glove."

I was stunned by the suddenness and fury of his rebuke.

"Come on," he commanded. He strode through the French doors and across the screened porch and down onto the lawn. I followed, smelling (with some pleasure) the oiled newness of the glove.

"All right," he said, "you stand over there." He waved me back—and back again, until I was about forty or fifty feet away. He tossed the ball up and rapped out a slow grounder. It went between my legs. I chased it down and threw it back. He one-handed the catch and tossed the ball and hit another grounder. It took a hop and caromed off beyond my stab with the glove. I laughed. He reddened.

"Get down on the ball! Use your body to stop it if necessary."

I stopped laughing. He was grim-faced. We went through the drill again and again until I managed to field most of the balls hit. And then he moved me farther back and began to hit under the ball, popping it up toward me. I was twelve. I was tall for my age and about as coordinated as a puppet with tangled strings.

At the end of an hour of this ordeal—for it had ceased to be any fun to me just minutes into it—he gave up. He handed me the bat and the ball and we went back into the house in silence. I went into my room and sat, trembling, on the bed, confused and angry.

At supper, Mother said something about a book she thought I would enjoy.

"Huh!" my father said. "Some boys enjoy playing with their fathers."

18

n the summer of that, my twelfth year, my father organized the grandest fishing expedition of his life. It is a tale of business, filial devotion, fish and fishing, good times, and maybe—just maybe—a penchant for self-destruction. It was also my redemption for my incredible ineptitude at the sport of baseball. (Why did he never want to join me in the fun of chipping those battered and cut gutta-percha balls at that peach basket? Why? "Fame talks about the where and when/while folly asks the why and wherefore . . ." the minor poet Winthrop Mackworth Praed wrote. I don't even know why I recollect that. I even had to look up his name.)

Daddy chartered a shrimp trawler (no other boats of suitable size were available for hire in those days) and invited a number of people to come along, including Uncle Boots from Charleston, Uncle Charles from Charlotte, and an Important Client. (Or two, according to a newspaper clipping, which I still have. There were five other men, whose names I recall, but whose business connections I do not.) I believe that some business deal of major importance hinged on his (their) happiness. In honor of the occasion, and perhaps to impress the client(s), Daddy bought a brand-new split-bamboo boat/surf rod and a new Penn Senator reel. I'm sure he envisioned the client holding this rod (enviously?) while struggling with a succession of large fish.

We left the shrimpboat dock next to the Lady's Island Bridge shortly after dawn one fine and hot Saturday morning in May (the 20th, 1949, to be precise), and proceeded downriver, past Beaufort's incomparable colonial waterfront, past Spanish Point, Port Royal, Parris Island, Land's End, and entered the swirling estuary, Port Royal Sound, that Jean Ribaut had sailed into four centuries earlier and become so enamored of. It was here, too, that the planter, politician, poet and sportsman William Elliott fished and wrote about it in his classic "Carolina Sports by Land and Water", published in 1846. (*"Bay Point, Aug. 17th, 1837. I give you a hasty narrative of an affair, which took place yesterday, between your humble servant and a Devilfish . . ."*)

The first thing we did was line up landmarks on Hilton Head Island and Bay Point for a supposedly choice spot called Hole-in-the-Wall. Modern NOAA charts show no particular drop-off in this area, but there is a peculiar, virtually inexplicable underwater hump called Middle Shoal, demarked just south of the ship's channel, right in the middle of the sound. Next to this—according to the chart—the depth does drop rather quickly to 44 feet, mean low water. Perhaps it was this for which we searched.

The shrimpboat captain set the anchor and we began to bottom-fish for bait, jigging dead shrimp for blackfish, catfish, or any small species.

These fish are then transferred to heavier tackle, hooked through the lips (blackfish) or despined and hooked through the dorsal area (catfish) and put out to free-swim, kept to the surface, or near it, by a cork float. Nowadays, the favored bait is live eels. But the principle is the same: cobia are astonishingly curious fish and will swim up to and around any floating object. Perhaps it is too anthropomorphic to say "curious"; maybe, as with dolphinfish, they like the shade—and because small fish and crabs are attracted to the relative sanctuary of this flotsam. The angling, then, is fairly lackadaisical. You sit, anchored, and wait for the cobia to show up, hopefully to be tempted by one of the morsels darting about apprehensively near the boat. (Less patient anglers, who seem to be prevalent today, cruise around the buoys and cast live bait to them, the way Southern Californians fish for broadbills.)

Cobia, also called ling in some areas, are common throughout the temperate waters of the world and begin showing up in Beaufort County as soon as the water temperature moderates. They probably congregate here to spawn.

We rocked gently in the groundswell that rolls in from the open Atlantic a scant mile or so distant, eating fried chicken and deviled eggs—all washed down by a little hair of the dog for the adults. I probably was allowed a sip or two of beer, given the loving nature of my uncles.

I was standing next to the beautiful split-bamboo rod, eating boiled peanuts and indulging in my usual fantasies. (Was I Zane Grey fishing off Tahiti in this instance?) Perhaps I merely dreamed of owning such a rig. Nevertheless, I was there when a very large cobia swam slowly up to the surface and eyed the terror-stricken blackfish bait with the air of a gourmand considering his supper in a restaurant tank.

"Daddy!" I yelled. "Cobia!"

Instinctively (today I would confess to "selfishly"), I picked up the rod. At the same moment, the cobia approached the blackfish, which probably had nearly expired from fright by now, and closed his big mouth over it. It all happened as if in slow motion—but that's the way cobia frequently bite. They almost never slash at a bait the way a bluefish would do, or a channel bass. One big yawning *gulp* and the cobia swallowed baitfish and hook and began to swim away in search of another easy meal. I reared back on the rod and drove the hook home in the fish's jaw.

Cobia are torpedo shaped and deceptively benign in demeanor. Their contours should be the first clue that they are very strong swimmers. As with the bigger, shyer, and similarly lethargic broadbill swordfish, they come alive when hooked.

Immediately, all rods were cleared away and the battle joined.

My father was in near hysterics, Uncle Boots was laughing, and the client probably poured himself another drink.

With any big fish, you have to play it to a certain extent, letting it do pretty much what it wants until it wears itself out, but all the while keeping it moving. (Hemingway was one of the pioneers of the modern style of "fighting" large fish and brought the first unmutilated giant bluefin tuna to the dock at Bimini in 1935.) This one wanted to swim—away from all this pain and annoyance. Only the flexibility of the rod, the stretch of the braided line, and the star drag on the reel, gave me a chance. At twelve, I probably weighed all of 120 pounds or so.

A number of times, the cobia circled the shrimp boat. The captain weighed anchor to reduce the possibility of snagging the line. Sometimes we drifted. At others, the captain started the engine and we trailed along behind the charging fish like some modern-day version of the Nantucket Sleighride. When the fish circumnavigated the trawler, I circled with it, walking along the side decks and around the high-pitched prow, Uncle Boots following, giggling, and holding me by the seat of my pants.

Daddy followed in our footsteps, pride and panic evident in voice and gesture.

It took us about half an hour to bring this fish to gaff. It was the only cobia we saw all day. It weighed—hours afterward on the shrimpboat dock—64 pounds. Not a state record, but a very big fish. Bill Culp from Palmetto Studios came down with his Speed Graphic and took a picture of me next to the dead fish, holding the split-bamboo rod like Hemingway on the docks at Alice Town. The fish was damned near as long as I was tall.

My father mailed the picture to *The News & Courier* in Charleston, which put it on the AP wire, and it got picked up by a lot of papers all over. Twenty years later, the prescient Andy Warhol got it right: I was famous for at least fifteen minutes—or however long it takes a man to read the sports section of the morning paper. E. Milby Burton, director of the Charleston Museum (the old one, the good one) even requested the picture for his archives.

Uncle Boots laughed about this for years to come, prancing around the room, pantomiming, playing all the parts, including my father. The tale became another staple of my family's oral tradition.

I have no idea what happened to the others. They may have slunk away, unnoticed, in the dockside celebration, although I'm sure they were gracious about it. I hope they had the good sense to come to the house for cobia steaks and homemade tartar sauce. I do know my father never recouped the family fortune. I have often wondered if this is what happened to the silver spoon.

19

For a brief period, I became a horse fancier—and owner, of sorts. I fell in love with the movies at a very early age and could be counted on to be at or near the front of the line for the Saturday matinee. Cartoon, serial, and a feature, usually a Western, sometimes (oh, most blessed of weekends) Tarzan. My celluloid hero, though, was Roy Rogers. (The name, obviously, was a big influence.) And it so happened that my godfather, William A. Campbell, Sr., owned Oak Grove Plantation at Sheldon, where he raised cattle and even employed the services of an honest-to-God wrangler or two on occasion. He gave me a horse, a marsh tacky (so named because they were said to be descended from horses that had escaped from the Spanish and lived wild in the salt marsh) called Hell's Bells. She was small, spirited, and stubborn. It was said that only Colin, Uncle Billy's youngest son, and I could ride her. For whatever reason, she was of not much use as a cow pony but I didn't care. She was mine. And Uncle Billy boarded her on the plantation for free. What a deal! (Once Mother came home and found me marking off a stall in the back yard where I intended to keep Hell's Bells.

After considerable heated wrangling of a different sort, the project was quashed.)

On the days when Daddy made a regular run to Walterboro to sell insurance, I'd take the school bus out to Oak Grove and ride until dusk. He would stop by on the way home, have a drink with Uncle Billy and Aunt Helen (and Bill, Jr. and Colin and their wives, Biz and Katie), and then take me home. Sometimes, I spent the weekend and took the school bus back into Beaufort on Monday morning.

Mother thought it quite elegant that I was learning to ride and sent me to the riding academy on Lady's Island for a spell. I was trained to an English seat and even rode in a few horse shows. This was not my style. I wanted to be out on the lone prairie (aka the lush pastures of Oak Grove), herding cattle or riding fence. Uncle Billy saved his copies of *The Quarterhorse Monthly* and other magazines pertaining to horses and the cattle business and I devoured them. I cut pictures of famous thoroughbreds out of magazines and made a scrapbook. I collected cheap statuettes. I sent away for Little Joe Wiesenfeld's tack catalog and daydreamed over the things I could never afford. I went with Uncle Billy to cattle auctions. I helped (in a very minor way) Colin break a quarterhorse named Moe.

Hell's Bells put up with my fantasies remarkably well. I used her in imaginary cattle drives, moving some of the white-faced Herefords around a little, fashioned a polo mallet out of a broomstick and whacked a tennis ball around, and led countless cavalry charges against Yankees or Indians through the oak and palmetto thickets. Hell's Bells extracted only one thing in retribution: if she were properly lathered up from all of this nonsense and she saw a puddle, she rolled in it. I learned in a hurry just to get the hell out of the saddle and let her roll.

Daddy was stoic.

In the end, he was right. My horse craziness lasted for about four years. It began to peter out as my interest in girls took a serious turn, and it finally dawned on me that horses were really stupid.

20

As was expected of me and any other ablebodied boy, I went out for junior-varsity sports. There was no Little League in Beaufort then. No pee wee football or any youthful training ground other than pickup games on The Green, where older boys usually left you with torn and grass-stained knickers and an abiding sense of curiosity—to wit: why am I doing this to myself? So it wasn't until I entered Beaufort Junior High School, which was merely a section of the old brick high school on Bay Street, that I was introduced to organized sport of any kind.

Frank Small was the JV coach. He was a short, muscular, athletic young man fresh out of Erskine College who loved kids, loved sports, and was adored in turn. For whatever reasons, I was assigned to become a fullback along with Louis Rabinowitz. So here in the heat of August afternoons, with the temperature stubbornly hovering in the high 90s and the sand gnats swarming by the billions, we were inducted into the warrior class. Some people thrive on it. I kept thinking how nicer it would be to be wading in the surf at Hunting Island, casting to anything—stingrays, catfish, clearnose skates . . . I didn't care. It was time for the spots to invade the rivers. There were flounder to be taken in the deep holes. The creeks were alive with shrimp and mullet.

Most of all, I hated tackling drills where inevitably I was the ball carrier and the biggest kid on the squad, Gunny Pyland, was the man I had to get by. Or through.

Daddy never missed a practice. His presence was the impelling force I needed, the spiritual cattle prod, as it were. ("Life without industry is guilt, industry without art is brutality. . . ." Had I but known Ruskin then!)

I suppose, like a lot of kids, I thought of quitting. But to have done so, of course, would have cast me in the role of pariah. It did not seriously enter my mind. Not then.

I made the team.

That might not seem so grand when you consider that Coach Small probably was a little short on boypower and warm bodies counted for much. I played not only fullback, but (in the days before specialization) linebacker, as well. I came to enjoy both positions. I was big for my age and at least could run straight into the line—into the Gunny Pyland of the opposition. Unfortunately, I was in my early twenties before I grew into my body and became fully coordinated. Oddly, I enjoyed playing linebacker most of all. It was very different when the ball carrier had to worry about me. Not that I was any big threat.

Of course, Daddy never missed a game, at home or away. (I don't think Mother ever came to any of them.) I remember my first game with embarrassing clarity. During warmups, the ends and backs formed two parallel lines and ran, two at a time, a simple pass pattern: you went out about ten yards and then cut toward the middle, crossing with the other player. The quarterback (Richard Ihly, who also was the star pitcher on the baseball team, and who later went to the Naval Academy) took the snap from the center (Juggy Hudson, one of many truly nice kids in that town) and passed to one of the intended receivers. On my first try, I was a little overwhelmed by the lights (football games usually were played at night in early fall in South Carolina because of the heat) and the noise of the crowd. I ran, made the cut, and looked expectantly back toward Richard—just in time to have the football hit me squarely in the face and send me sprawling. We wore no face guards then. I was lucky it didn't knock out any teeth. My cheeks stung, but mostly with shame.

If Coach Small saw the gaffe, he never said anything. In fact, I started the game as the deep man on the receiving squad. I saw the kickoff coming end-over-end against the insect-filled haloes of the lights, saw it bounce on the turf and hobble toward me. I ran to meet it, scooped it up (no mistake here!) and began to follow my blockers toward the left side of the middle of the field. Textbook.

The next thing I knew, Juggy was tugging at my jersey, saying: "Roy . . . over here. The huddle's over here . . ."

I'd been blindsided by a John's Island tackler. Whole solar systems whirled in front of my eyes.

My father throve on this, my very modest athleticism. Sometimes I'd look over at the sidelines and see him march behind Coach Small, in lockstep, like some Mutt-and-Jeff dance team. After the games, he'd gather all the cheerleaders and buy them Cokes and hot dogs.

Mine was not, however, a brilliant football career. I never scored a touchdown; that was left pretty much to our halfbacks, Jimmy Polk and Richard Bell, and the ends—and Louis Rabinowitz. The proudest moment I had was once when, after the whistle had blown, I was still digging and squirming, like some mole, trying to get through the mud-smeared, smelly mound of the defense, trying desperately to get into the end zone. One of the referees picked me up by the scruff of my jersey and said, "That's the way to do it, son. Keep fightin'."

In winter, we moved on to basketball. Again, because of my height (all of about 6'1") I found myself alternating as center with Murray Connelly. A 6'1" point guard today would be considered small. I'm sure I looked like the scarecrow in *The Wizard of Oz* when I tried to dribble downcourt. I developed only one shot worth mentioning: a flat-footed, two-handed, extremely low-trajectory heave from the very corner—slightly behind the backboard. (It was the only shot I could use to get points against Coach Small in those impromptu games of

Horse we played after practice.) Although—and this memory astonishes me—I could hit an old-fashioned hook shot with either hand. There was no real touch involved; they were caroms off the glass—or boards, as it were. Perhaps this shouldn't surprise me today because I discovered—much too late to do any good for the beleaguered Tidal Wave—that I bat best lefty. I don't know why. Anything else I attempt with my left arm seems to go awry.

In any event, I didn't score much. Because of my height, Head Coach Alan Shelton had me work out some with the varsity, but that came to naught. I wasn't ready. But I did earn my letter and the scarlet woolen sweater on which to display it.

Daddy, who by now was deeply involved in the vestry at St. Helena's Episcopal Church, must have thought God was taking a personal interest in him. His son was a junior jock.

It didn't last.

21

A*dolescence and I* collided like electrons in a particle accelerator. Hormones, rebellion, frustration, anxiety, manifested in the peculiarly ambivalent result that we all regard as unique.

By my freshman year in high school, Daddy's business had taken a serious downturn amidst an expanding town and a thriving economy. I think he simply was not a good salesman. I love him still, but I think I can say this without attracting thunderbolts. Mother was still working, as a secretary in Uncle Herbert's office, but money was a problem. Aunt Helen (Albrecht) sent down some of Cousin Pete's old clothes. I wore a pair of his pants to a party one night and was laughed at, because they clearly belonged to an earlier era. I was humiliated in that particularly hurtful way that scars young people so deeply. I quit all athletics and took a job as an usher and popcorn seller at the Breeze Theater. The manager of the theater was a chain-smoking, soft-spoken man named Bacot Alston, who understood the nature of fractious youth and dealt with us (me, Charles Godley and Oliver McEachern) with patience and compassion. We would have done anything for him.

Daddy was heartbroken. He, too, was humiliated—by his own failure to provide for me and by the evaporation of his most cherished dream for me, the athletic career.

On Sundays I was the devout, God-fearing acolyte at St. Helena's. Other days, I wore pegged pants, combed my hair in a drake's ass, sneaked cigarettes and beer, and started to hang around the pool hall behind Harvey's Barber Shop.

My father's reaction to this was equally baffling—in consequence, perhaps supremely compassionate. He deplored the clothing, but gave me written permission to play pool (Furman Harvey required it of anybody under sixteen) as long as I didn't wager money on the games. I honored that request. I also spent an awful lot of time leaning over these green baize playing fields, practicing bank shots, deeply immersed in the strategies of straight pool, rotation, eight ball, and the rest. A hustler named Dynamite taught me a number of trick shots.

But my descent into a form of social anarchy did not include criminality. I did have a job. I'd always—since the entreprenurial days of smashing flies at a penny apiece—done odd jobs to supplement my allowance: I ran a neighborhood lawn-mowing service at a buck-fifty per yard. I bought my first two cameras with the proceeds.

My overt rebellion lasted only several years. By the time I was fourteen and had my driver's license (that was the permissible age in South Carolina then; it had to do with being a largely agricultural state and farm boys needed to drive at an early age) I began to date. By degrees, I shed the trappings of the nascent hoodlum and began to adopt the costume of the 1950s: T-shirt, Levi's, black penny loafers, and white athletic socks—or, later, the James Dean look of Jack Purcells, chinos, and sweat shirt.

I enjoyed the freedom that having a regular salary gave me. I bought most of my own clothes, paid for my own dates (I gave up the allowance), and contributed to gasoline for a 1949 Plymouth coupe that I shared with mother. She drove it to work by day; at night it was my rod. I installed a piercing "wolf whistle" that operated off the exhaust manifold and was manipulated by a wire under the dashboard.

Life, as I entered high school, was pretty much something out of the movies: Hollywood's vision of the American Dream, Middle-class Division, Whiteboy Department. I was Mickey Rooney (a taller Mickey Rooney and without the freckles) to a succession of Judy Garlands. There were sock hops in the gym after every football or basketball game. There were hayrides to Hunting Island. We dated. I mean, really dated: you took a bath, put on your cleanest shirt and pants, drove to the girl's house, endured the agonizing scrutiny of her parents, siblings, aunts, uncles, cousins, and neighbors, worried that her dog might try to hump your leg (the ultimate mortification), and then took the girl, who probably was equally as tense and abashed, to the movies and, afterward, to The Shack or Al's for a cheeseburger and a shake (the little black boys who worked as carhops would bring you a beer in a milkshake cup, if you really wanted one; this subterfuge always seemed to either fool—or placate—the police) and then, if you were really lucky, you'd drive up to Bay Street and park down the grassy slope under one of the old live oaks—Beaufort Bay a shimmering mirage of moonlight—and neck. Very few ever got any luckier than that. But it earned you bragging rights of sorts in the locker room during PE.

I did give athletics one last try. In addition to chipping golf balls at the peach basket, I began to throw a baseball against one of the brick pillars of the house. I'd paced off the proper distance to an imaginary pitcher's mound and pretended that the pillar was the strike zone. Ultimately, I wore out several baseballs throwing them against the bricks. I even developed a side-arm slider that actually broke now and then and a knuckleball that sometimes dipped at the "plate," but my fastball was a good excuse for any batter to go take a leak while he waited for it to arrive, and my change-up was any pitch I didn't mean to throw, which was most.

With all good intentions, I went out for the varsity baseball team. Our coach that year was a large, bald man who looked like Curly of The Three Stooges. He was one of those itinerant teachers who drift through schools for a year and move on. He was hot tempered and shifted players around like Chinese checkers. My pitching career lasted one tryout. After that, I caught batting practice a few times, but my peg to second almost had to be relayed by the pitcher. I was consigned to the outfield. Center field, to be exact. Again, anytime a long fly ball was hit toward me, the second baseman would begin to sprint out for a certain relay.

We played our games on the old diamond at the defunct Naval Air Station, which had been opened up by the county as a sort of industrial park. (I don't think it attracted much industry, and eventually the Marine Corps took it over again as an active field.) On our very first road trip, about half the team bought chewing tobacco, the better to emulate their big-league heroes, and spent most of the ensuing game sprawled belly down on the bench, retching into the fresh spring grasses. I wore number 7. I got to play intermittently. I think we were 0–11 that year.

This gave Daddy one short season of renewed hope. He bought me a new fielder's glove and a brand-new pair of baseball shoes. More than that, he invested his very soul in me, in my clumsy efforts to please him. Ultimately, I was to let him down yet again. At the end of the year, I tossed the glove into the top of my closet and sold my spikes to Pat Dennis. I never played organized sports again.

Daddy was desperate. I attended all of Beaufort High's games—by now as the sports editor of the *Tidal Wave*, the BHS monthly newspaper, as sportswriter for *The Beaufort Gazette*, and as a special correspondent for *The News & Courier* in Charleston and *The State* in Columbia. But that was not enough for him. He took me to football games at Parris Island. And baseball games at Parris Island. He lectured me on the finer points of strategy. I used this expanding knowledge in my stories, but I never played again.

Writing for the *Gazette* nearly ruined me as a journalist. Howard Cooper paid me 10 cents a column inch. I could take a Friday-night football game and turn it into *War and Peace*.

Under the influence of several teachers, I flourished academically. Mrs. Cecile Gray, who taught mathematics, was such a wonderful teacher that I took every course she offered and managed to get As and A+s. In the eighth grade, I think it was, I had come under the influence of a Mrs. Kermit Andrus (her given name is not listed in my old yearbooks), whose sharp mind stimulated my own. (I even won the Eighth Grade Spelling Bee, which flabbergasted my mother. When I showed her the $1.50 I'd won, she said: "And this from the boy who spells Bible, b-i-b-a-l?") In the latter years, I was fortunate enough to study English under Mrs. Mary Vella and Latin, English, and journalism under Mrs. Virlie V. Holmes. I will never forget sitting in Mary Vella's classroom and having T. W. Eatmon, our principal, read aloud a short story I had written and praise it lavishly. I was embarrassed, as all teenagers are at such public display, but hugely pleased as well. Unfortunately, the story did not win a prize in the state literary contest. Maybe the subject matter—cannibalism—had something to do with that. Mrs. Holmes, I learned later in life, when it became my profession, taught an excellent course in journalism.

There were other fine teachers, some of whom I knew by reputation, but took no classes under. And there were, sad to mention, many who were incompetent. I remember correcting my tenth-grade English teacher's pronunciation.

My social life was pretty full. Somehow I managed to catch the eye of the beautiful and charming Jerry Sample, who was a year ahead of me. She managed my political campaigns and got me elected president of the sophomore and junior classes. (Alas, Jimmy Polk thrashed me in the contest for senior-class president; politicians, it seems—even in high school—begin to smell a little after two terms.) Miss Margaret Geraldine, who set a standard by which all women have been measured since (in apostrophe to wives past and present: you measured up, okay?), became my more-or-less-steady girlfriend. Unfortunately, when she went away to college, she discovered midshipmen from Annapolis—college men; not highschool boys. *Sic transit gloria LeRoy.* In compensation, however, I met the lovely Jane Scott Brown, whose father was a navy captain and a doctor at Parris Island.

When the owners of the Breeze Theater built the new Royal Drive-In Theater, I moved out there and became assistant manager. Not too long after, the theaters were sold and I took a job processing black-and-white film at Palmetto Studios. And, late in my junior year, Beaufort got its first radio station, 1,000-watt WBEU. We knew then that our little town had moved into the mainstream. We weren't hicks no mo'.

I was one of a number of kids asked to audition for a Saturday-morning teen-time show on WBEU and was selected as cohost along with Louisa Simmons, a perky, bright-eyed young lady who was generously decorated with *taches de rousseur* (freckles, to you). The show was called "Teen Time with Roy and Louisa." We read news clips of school activities and played musical requests. I discovered that I had a certain talent for the broadcast business. That is, a mellifluence of voice and a sense of timing. I was quickly offered a part-time job as an announcer. I worked from 3:30 in the afternoon until sign-off (sundown by FCC law, which meant that the time changed every single day of the year), and a full shift on Saturdays.

But, for all of this, the water remained my locus and focus. Poopy had moved to Columbia, when his father was promoted by South Carolina Electric and Gas; but other friends, including a new one, Jimmy Murray, and I made regular jaunts to Hunting Island to fish in the surf (the south end of Hunting Island also was a wonderful place to take a girlfriend because it was so deserted) or from docks, or from a boat—anybody's boat.

My father and I reached a truce, of sorts. A regular byline in the newspaper and a voice on the radio gave me a minor notoriety—if not celebrity—of which he was passably proud. But we were, ineluctably, drawing apart as parent and child always will do at that stage. He loved the music of his young manhood and sang "Peg o' My Heart" or "Daisy." He read *Time, Life, Collier's,* and *The Saturday Evening Post.* I listened to rhythm and blues on WLAC in Nashville late every night and my music was "Honey Love," "Rock Around the Clock," and the banished-but-beloved cult classics like "Annie Had a Baby" and "Baby Lemme Bang Yo' Box." I devoured periodicals, too, but was well into Joyce, Hemingway, O'Hara, Stein, Sartre, Camus, and about to plunge into the world of Kerouac, Ginsberg, Ferlinghetti, Ionesco, Beckett, and the rest.

My fledgling literary efforts already had attracted the attention of several of Beaufort's resident and seasonal salons. Ann Head (ex-wife of sporting goods mogul Howard Head) first read my short stories. She was Beaufort's leading celebrity, as she wrote fiction regularly for *The Saturday Evening Post, Redbook,* and other national magazines. Ann then passed them on to the prolific writer Samuel Hopkins Adams (who wrote, among other things, "It Happened One Night," which was made into the famous movie starring Clark Gable and Claudette Colbert), who wintered in Beaufort in a house on Battery Creek. Sam, in turn, showed them to the poet Carl Carmer. All of them encouraged me to continue. Sam gave me two wonderful pieces of advice:

"One sonofabitch on a page is enough." (Meaning, obviously, that strong language loses its punch if repeated too often.)

And:

"You have to believe, when you sit at the typewriter, that what you are writing is the greatest thing ever put on paper.

"Of course," he added, "the next day you'll ball it up and throw it away, but . . ."

22

The gulf widened and threatened Daddy and me. Nothing about this is preternatural; if anything, it is all too familiar. He had little to say, that I remember, about my writing. I do clearly remember his comment on my photography: "Roy takes good pictures, but he takes too damned many of them."

One year he took me to Augusta to see The Masters and in the huge, swirling galleries of the Augusta National Golf Club, I quickly became separated from him. I did not find him until late that afternoon, when we met back at the car. I was alarmed and upset. He was furious. "Next time," he said acidly, "I'm coming with somebody who wants to be with me."

No explanation would ameliorate the situation or exonerate me. I can still see the look on his face.

Late in my junior year, my parents sold the house on Pigeon Point and bought several lots from my Uncle Herbert on Lady's Island. In a sense, this transaction was all too typical of my father's lack of business acumen. Earlier, he had had an opportunity to buy something like twenty acres (perhaps in partnership with Uncle Herbert; I don't remember), but declined, because he thought the property, which followed the contours of Rock Springs Creek, was too far from town. Only a year or two later, he wound up paying about the same amount for a fraction of the property. Nevertheless, the lots were situated on a high bluff and were shaded by huge live oaks and one magnificent black hickory tree. They began to build their retirement cottage, a modest one-story house with only two bedrooms and a bath and a half, a study/office for my father, a pleasant eat-in kitchen, and a screened porch. It fulfilled the basic needs of any Lowcountry native. Havilah Babcock, a professor of English at the University of South Carolina and the author of many stories on fishing and hunting, wrote that all any real South Carolinian ever wanted was to be elected to the state legislature and have his own fishing pond. Transpose that to the Lowcountry and change it to a house on a deep creek and a private dock, and you have exactly how we Beaufort Countians feel.

Temporarily, we rented a house in a section of Beaufort called Harvey's Bottom. It was an old farmhouse in rickety condition. (I once was awakened in the night by someone tousling my hair. It turned out to be a rat. I chased it out onto the screened porch and killed it with an antique French bayonet.) While we "camped" here, as Mother put it, there was one other event of potential momentousness, bordering on possible disaster: my cousin Patsy, the ex-brat, came to live with us for a few months. By now she was sixteen and utterly gorgeous, with ringlets of fiery auburn, eyes the color of a bonefish flat on a cloudless morning, and the figure any Hollywood starlet would (and usually did) pay a fortune to possess. Patsy and I began to take more appreciative looks at each other. Mother quickly sniffed the heady scent of scandal in the family and dispatched poor Patsy back to Key West.

The summer before my senior year, we moved into the new house on Lady's Island. Mother promptly gave license to her romanticism and dubbed the place Cove Creek.

One day she went to the Beaufort County Jail and picked up several trusties and drove them out to Lady's Island. They were to help clear the underbrush from the bluff. She went back into town to her job (by then as visiting teacher for the county). When she returned at lunch, she found that no brush had been cleared but my father had recruited their help in building a dock!

My father was very proud that I was going to college. He fussed and fumed about tuition and fees (his business was going through yet another dip) and reiterated his bitterness over the fact that his twin, Fred, had received higher education while he had not. There was always the intimation that he had stayed behind and worked in the store at Sheldon and put Fred through college. This always had the faint odor of sour grapes, given his predilections. Although the family's fortunes were in decline steadily after Grandfather John Kansas Attaway's death, intuition tells me that Daddy simply did not want to go to college until it was too late.

I applied to the Universities of Virginia and North Carolina, although my deepest desire was to go to Princeton. I didn't even think about applying there. I assumed that any Ivy League school was well out of mine. (Another oddity: Daddy refused to send me to the University of South Carolina or Clemson, claiming they were inferior. Why he thought this, that is to say, what his criteria were, I cannot fathom. But he was adamant.) I was convinced that no school of Princeton's reputation would even consider me, even though I had excellent grades and SATs. I knew only that Daddy did not have the wherewithal to send me anywhere without some form of help.

As it was, both UVA and UNC accepted me and in July of that summer, 1955, I decided to become a Tar Heel. It was a decision that I have never regretted. Twenty-some-odd years later I saw the Princeton campus for the first time and inexplicably burst into tears. Some ancient hurt manifested itself, but vanished, was exorcised, in that brief moment of grief for a desire unrequited. But someone once remarked that you don't so much attend the University of North Carolina as become a convert to it. It is true. For God so loved the Tar Heels, he painted the sky Carolina blue. And Dean Smith is His apostle.

I approached college with the naïveté and high-blown ideals (Byronic claptrap, you might think) that have characterized my approach to life for half a century. To me, Chapel Hill loomed as a sacrosanct temple of learning. I would sit at the feet of professors who were filled with the love of teaching who would take the time to nurture my so-tender psyche. They would water the buds of my intellectualism and smile as it flourished. (Honest, I really believed this stuff, but not in such baroque terms; hyperbole here, to make a point.) Thomas Wolfe was one of the university's most illustrious literary products. I read all of his novels that summer before matriculating. I would be his spiritual heir. (Mother fostered this notion; Daddy recited the statistics and heroics of Charlie "Choo-Choo" Justice, one of Carolina's greatest football players. He hadn't given up yet.)

Further, I was placed in an advanced program, effectively going straight into my sophomore year. The only freshman course I was required to take was one in general health and hygiene, taught by an assistant coach. During his droning lectures on food groups and soap, we all read *The Daily Tar Heel* and drank coffee or worked on assignments for our next classes; if you knew enough to brush your teeth after eating, you could pass.

I was, naturally, stunned by the cynicism, the sheer indifference to teaching that manifested itself amongst the faculty. I damned near flunked out of school my first semester. Only a bout with mumps and meningitis and concomitant lengthy stay in the university's medical-school hospital saved me; I was given another shot at the skewed courses and did much better. (I did have several wonderful professors; they weren't all concerned solely with tenure track or fat and lazy as the result of having attained it.)

In the midst of this confusion, I was otherwise having a hell of a good time. Party Boy Roy. My first roommates in Alexander dorm were an ex-navy enlisted man and some fat farm kid from eastern North Carolina. (We were in a large corner room.) The ex-serviceman I got along with fine; the fat kid should have gone to N. C. State. In the adjacent room were two other boys who weren't exactly simpatico, either: a scrawny sex- and sartorially obsessed boy and an energetic kid from Pottstown, Pennsylvania, named John Hunnicutt, who had come to Carolina from the Hill School. About two weeks into our first semester, John and I discussed our roommates over a couple of beers at The Rat and came to the conclusion that we should be roomies and be rid of our others. That Saturday, when the two North Carolina natives had gone home for the weekend, John and I switched personal effects around, putting the fat kid and the scrawny kid in together. When they came back to the dorm Sunday evening, we told them the university had made a mistake and that these were the proper room assignments. They never questioned it.

John Hunnicutt and I became lifelong friends. We pledged the same fraternity, Chi Psi, and were both Naval ROTC cadets. He was even my best man—the second time around, when I married the former Miss Robyn Worth Gill of Chicago in 1982.

John's family was transferred to California, putting them out of reach for anything but the lengthiest of holidays, and he became a regular visitor to the Attaway household at the new house on Lady's Island. My father took it as some sort of sign: his own son was obsessed with girls and awful music; John was a polite and willing temporary substitute. Besides, John had been a wrestler in prep school and was more athletically attuned, meaning: he could (and would) discuss baseball. I was a novitiate in the temple of Tar Heel basketball, but that didn't count. The first time John came to visit was at Thanksgiving. Our first morning there, Daddy came into our bedroom and wanted to know whether anybody wanted to go fishing. (Trout season was in full swing.) John dutifully got out of bed and accompanied him. I lounged for hours, dozing and dreaming. Daddy was incensed. At lunch he made some caustic comment that angered me so I refused to go fishing with him the rest of the holiday.

Meanwhile, I was descending into what may have been a premature mid-life crisis. Both parents sensed it. Uncle Boots even wrote a letter (obviously at my parents' urging), trying to rally me.

"Son," he wrote in part, "you have hot pants . . ."

Well, that may have been part of the problem. Essentially,

I was one of those kids who should have enlisted in the armed services first, had some sense kicked into his head, undergone at least a modicum of maturation, and then gone to college.

Mother continued to write letters of encouragement and was living vicariously through my own intellectual forays. Daddy's approach was more pragmatic:

> "I am attaching the check for $85.00 for your initiation charges and am sending it Special delivery so that it will reach you by Monday. Why did you wait so late to let me know about this extra amount needed? Surely you must have known it was coming up and what it would amount to therefore I should have known about it earlier. As you know, my bank account is such that I have to anticipate money needed in advance and then try to provide it. Small amounts are alright but to me $85.00 is no small amount and the last you said about this was that it could be paid by you in installments, however, here it is. I am also sending a check for $89.00 for your house bill but YOU DID NOT SEND THE BILL IN YOUR LETTER AND I AM NOT SURE THIS IS CORRECT AMOUNT . . . In any event be sure that you send me the house bill and please let them know up there that you are careless about getting it to me."
>
> (From a letter dated March 6, 1956.)

Originally, my allowance had been $10 per week. That had been cut to $7.50. Things were very tight. By now, I was working as one of the few paid student announcers at WUNC-TV, the university's own Channel 4, earning about $10 a week for such regular duties.

In the middle of that tumultuous freshman year, Jane Scott Brown and I were married—secretly. She was at Queen's College in Charlotte, and I spent many a weekend hitchhiking down to see her, staying with my Uncle Charles and Aunt Bryte. His son, my cousin Bucky, who is two days younger than I, was playing football at the University of South Carolina. (Something of which my father took pains to remind me when the occasion arose—which it did frequently.) One Saturday, I borrowed Uncle Charles's car and Jane and I drove to York, South Carolina, a notorious marriage mill, and were married by a justice of the peace. I had been writing letters for some time, trying to prepare the family for this. On December 2, Mother wrote:

> "Dear Son:
>
> I have just finished reading your letter for the second time, and while parts of it transported me to thrilling heights, parts depressed me very much, and what you *didn't* say left me with a feeling of *void*.
>
> "... I liked what you said about Jane. Everyone needs someone (I can just see you tear your hair over my triteness—if the Navy has left enough of it. But you know what I mean.) You never really told me before; not that you needed to especially, but I'm glad you did. The reason she is such a good safety valve for you is that she loves you. Just remember your forebears' motto 'Noblesse Oblige.' I don't care how mad you get with me, just *remember.* We'll probably resume this discussion when you get home. Just leave all sarcasm up there in the hills, and sharpen your *long range* ambitions on the grindstone of whatever stimuli appear."

Apparently I had written a poem (which—perhaps mercifully—does not survive) about a leaf about to fall. She went on to say:

> "Like your leaf, you are mentally walking something of a tightrope, but you will make it. "

On March 5 she wrote:

> "Dearest Son:
>
> We got your much-looked-for letter this morning, and so glad to hear from you—but why in heck can't you mention, or answer some of the things I say? I just wanted to have you reply to some of the things you asked me— natural, eh? ... I was worried when I called, darling, but I didn't beat around the bush. I just wanted to know first-hand how you were. And, as I told you, Daddy is not too well. He is really better now tho, than when I called. Has taken his usual spring tonic of quinine etc. Also, he is on

the trail of a timber deal. If it works out, he will then feel fine!

By the end of the school year in 1956, Jane was pregnant. We went back to Beaufort and told our parents. They were devastated.

If anybody understood this, it probably was Uncle Charles. Bucky had gotten married at fourteen. We tended to do that sort of thing in the South. To his and Vickie's credit, they're still married.

23

For a couple of years, I worked in radio, first in Beaufort at WBEU (we lived with Jane's parents on Parris Island) and then at WALD in Walterboro, where our first daughter was born. She was delivered by Dr. Riddick Ackerman, Jr., son of the man who delivered me. In a well-meaning but amazing burst of idiocy, we decided to name her after both grandmothers. Thus she was named Dorothy Claire. And then we realized we couldn't possibly call her by one name or the other because it would infuriate the one left out. And we didn't want her to grow up as just another damned double-name southern belle. As a joke, I remarked, "She squalls so much, maybe we should call her 'Stormy'."

It stuck. My mother hated it and called her Miss Boo (which we hated and refused to acknowledge). Stormy liked it, though. Today she teaches at the College of Engineering of Boston University, and that's what it says on her office door: Prof. Stormy Attaway. (I'm constrained to remark that the operative verb here is "teaches"; she effectively removed herself from tenure track because she wants to devote her energies to teaching instead of pursuing grants.) She is married to another professor, Ted DeWinter.

Eventually we moved back to Beaufort and WBEU again. I learned something very quickly about small-town radio: every time you asked for a raise, they told you how great you were and gave you a new title in lieu of. At one time, I was chief announcer, program director, and news director. I sold spots on the side.

Meanwhile, we had a second daughter, Catherine Jane, an energetic and affectionate child. She is now in the film business in Atlanta. She was named for nobody in particular, plus her mother. We took no chances. She is known by the simple diminutive "Cathy," to which nobody could object.

And, as usual, my "career" at this point resembled nothing so much as a ball in a pinball machine. Radio was fine, it was a lot of fun (at Carolina I had done radio drama—which had not yet died out) but I wanted to write.

Over the next four years, I worked variously as a substitute clerk-carrier for the post office, sold men's clothing for Schein's Department Store, and worked as a handyman for the local Sears Roebuck & Co. catalog store. Two of these jobs were perfect for a budding writer. At the post office, I filled in where needed, substituting for the carriers when they were sick or on vacation. Eventually, I became the parcel-post delivery-man—for the entire town. (That's how small Beaufort was then.) In the course of this job, sooner or later I got to knock on the door of every house within the corporate limits. I also worked, in that department, with the Rev. Willie Smith, called "Deacon" by everyone, a black minister whose passions in life were Gullah spirituals and fishing for (and eating) drumfish.

Deacon claimed to have the original version of the spiritual about the Storm of '93, part of which went:

"Oh, de wind did blow so hard,
De storm was all abroad;
And yet we recognize in it
De wonderful power of Gawd . . ."

My father had sung it to me as a lullaby.

Working at Sears was even more fun—for a while. My first job there was helping the handyman and sweeping the floor. This was even better than working at the post office because, when the handyman went to install an air conditioner or some other household appliance, I went along and we actually got inside the houses. Now I was glimpsing how people, black and white, lived in every conceivable social stratum.

But there was a problem.

The manager of the Sears Catalog Store was a short, red-faced young man named Bobby. He was very proud of being a store manager.

One day, on my lunch break, I was sitting on some cartons in the storeroom in back of the store, eating a sandwich and reading a book. I think it was *Le Rouge et Le Noir*. Bobby came in.

"Whatchu doin', boy?"

"Having lunch." I shrugged.

He looked at me, at the sandwich, and then at the paperback in my hands.

"Readin' a book?"

"Yessir."

"Whatchu readin'?"

"A novel. A French novel."

He grinned suspiciously and left without another word.

About a week later, he called me into his office.

"You know, I been thinkin' about you," he said. "You got a little education, ain't you?"

"Not much," I said.

"Well, you don't belong back here, sweepin' and puttin' together bicycles and lawn mowers and stuff. I'mo move you up into the credit department."

I protested vociferously. To no avail. My blue collar was exchanged for a white one, and I found myself in the front office, posting accounts along with two ladies. Although not as much fun as my previous job, it was okay. It was sufficiently mindless work that I could still think mostly about writing.

Several months later, Bobby called me into his office again.

"You know," he began, "so-and-so's husband done been transferred to California [one of the ladies' husbands was a jet mechanic at the Marine Corps Air Station], and I need somebody to take over the credit department. I'mo send you to credit manager's school, and when you come out, you'll be the boss in there!"

He was beaming, anticipating my humble gratitude. His face crumbled when I declined, reiterating that I really wanted to go back to my job as assistant handyman.

Another week or so went by. He summoned me to his office yet again.

"I been thinkin' about it," Bobby said. "And you know, you're right, in a sense. Bein' a credit manager's a real borin' job ain't it?"

"Yessir."

"I don't blame you. But I done thought it over, and what I'mo do is send you to *manager's* school and when you come out, you'll be the manager of your own Sears Catalog Store . . . just like me!"

My heart died for a moment. I knew what this meant to him. But again I was forced to decline his offer. When I left his office, he was scowling.

The next day, he summoned me one more time.

"This's been vexin' me," he said. "I offered to send you to credit manager's school, and you turned me down. Now, I understood that one. But then I offered to send you to manager's school, and you turned that one down!"

He leaned across his gray metal desk. I tried to transport myself out of the moment by trying to remember on which page it could be found in the catalog. Bobby was as red-faced as a St. Helena Island tomato in June.

"I ain't never met a man with so little ambition," he said slowly. "I'mo do you a big favor, boy, wake you up. I'mo fire you."

And he did.

24

My *parents and* Jane's were always cordial to each other—within a certain framework. Jane's father was completely acceptable because he was a North Carolinian, the son of the famous Mountain Doctor, James Steven Brown, Sr., whose death prompted front-page stories in most of that state's newspapers. Captain Brown was a short, trim and fit man whose very presence—especially in uniform with four gold stripes on each sleeve—commanded attention and respect, despite his diminutive size. He was a brilliant man in many ways, Phi Beta Kappa at Davidson College and a graduate of Tulane Medical School. He was a member of the American College of Surgeons. For a time, he had practiced medicine in Hendersonville, the family seat, and once took out his own appendix under a local anesthetic while his fellow surgeons stood around and watched and laughed. It was said he joined the navy in World War II to get away from his mother-in-law. I think he just liked adventure and moving around. Hendersonville was too small for him. Perhaps his own father cast too long a shadow. During the war, he duplicated his self-help surgery by performing a hernia operation on himself on a hospital ship. He was that kind of a man. He also loved to fish.

Jane's mother, whom her father had met in the South Pacific while he was working as a ship's doctor and she was on a cruise to get over a failed first marriage, was—how can I put it gently?—a Yankee. Heaven forfend. She was the former Dorothy Beaver, of a prominent New York City family (there is a Beaver Street in lower Manhattan), who spoke out with the bluntness of her upbringing. Southerners, mind you, will tell you what kind of a stupid lowlife you are, but will do so in such courteous terms that it's only much later you realize you've been insulted. Dot Brown came right to the point.

Jane (after the unfortunate and predictable acrimony of divorce had dissipated, she became a very good friend of Robyn's and mine; Robyn had nothing to do with the breakup) told me recently that her "take" on the situation was this: both of her parents liked my father a lot; my father, in turn, liked them; Dr. Brown was very fond of my mother; my mother and Jane's mother circled each other warily.

"I always felt," Jane said, "that if your father died and my mother died, my father and your mother would somehow get together."

She also said that she thought my father adored my mother but that Mother tolerated him. In retrospect, this makes sense.

Jane's mother and I also had a serious row—a seething disagreement that finally erupted—that left us not speaking to each other for about a year. In the end, we became dear friends. Many years later, when she was in a nursing home on Hilton Head Island, I went to see her. After I left her room, and as I was walking down the polished hallway, a quavering voice followed me:

"I love you," it said.

I ran back to her, and we embraced. I told her I loved her, too. It was the last time I saw her.

So, our families, which had been very nice to each other during our dating days, suddenly found themselves linked by marriage and not altogether happy about it. I understood the depth of that feeling when one evening my parents came over to the Browns' quarters for supper. While we were having drinks beforehand, I took Daddy by the arm and said, "Come on, I want to show you something."

I led him out to the laundry room off the kitchen and showed him Captain Brown's fishing rods, all brand-new, top-of-the-line spinning gear, all neatly arrayed in special racks. Daddy spun at me.

"I don't want to see his goddamn rods!" he snapped.

25

*I*f *I had* disappointed Daddy again, having grandchildren made him extremely happy. He doted on the girls, Stormy and Cathy. He came by to see them every single day. He took them for rides and bought them candy and ice cream. He dandled and hugged them, and you could see the affection and pride on his face.

And we began to fish together again.

Many Sundays, when he didn't have to be an usher at the eleven o'clock service, we would go to the early service and then rush into our fishing clothes and be off to whatever creek rumor had it was hot at the moment.

In 1959 I went back to school briefly, attending summer sessions in Chapel Hill. Jane and the girls stayed with the Browns, who by now had been transferred to the Philadelphia Navy Yard. At the end of the summer, we ran out of money. The Browns were preoccupied with keeping Jane's brother Jimmy in college. My father's business was in yet another downward spiral. While digging through family archives for this book, I found one telling artifact: There was a birthday card to me (September 1959) with a check for $100 inside. It had never been cashed. I probably knew he couldn't cover it.

I came back to Beaufort and took a job working for Howard Cooper at the *Beaufort Gazette*, determined yet to write—for anyone, anywhere. The writing was the disease, at times a chore, but always the one thing that could satisfy whatever it is that harries and sorrows the soul. It is a compulsion, a necessity, and—not infrequently—an exorcism of personal ghosts.

Howard Cooper was a brilliant man, a reporter able to grasp the nuances of a situation and distill them into a comprehensible story. He was also cheap. Parsimonious. Penurious. Cheap. He knew a desperate disciple when he saw one. He no longer paid me ten cents a column inch. I was salaried: $15 per week.

The *Gazette* was then still in its old quarters on Charles Street. The staff consisted of Howard Cooper, Mrs. Black, who was society editor and anything else she needed to be (the first rule of weekly newspapering is: the more names you include, the more copies you sell), Bacot Alston (who had quit the theater business and was the *Gazette*'s advertising director) and me—the ultimate swing man. I sold ads, I wrote sports and general features and news, and learned to run a Linotype machine and Miehle and Heidelberg job presses. In the parlance of the newspaper business, I was a printer's devil. The composing-room crew consisted of a toothless old man, a hapless and helpless alcoholic whose very pores reeked of vile poison and who ate candy all day to satisfy the craving for whiskey's sugar. There also usually was some itinerant printer who would stay with us until the whiskey whisked him away again; a lady whose name I cannot remember, who ran one of the Linotypes (and who used to compose stories about her and her friends and their parties and drop them into the society columns unbeknownst to Mrs. Black); Howard's brother Rudy, an amiable jack-of-all-trades; and our pressman, a black kid named Brooks, who was about my age, maybe a year or two older. As the paper began to expand, Hugh Gibson, a retired

Marine Corps journalist, joined the team. (Hugh was a wonderful, graceful writer and later became *The News & Courier's* ace political reporter in Columbia.) On press nights (Wednesday), everybody put on old clothes and pitched in.

The press Brooks had to run was an old flatbed, sheetfed Babcock. The paper was printed in eight-page sections on both sides of large, cut sheets of newsprint. It was printed four pages at a time, and then the pages had to be turned over and the other four pages printed on the obverse side. The worst part was that Brooks had to sit and feed each sheet individually into the roaring maw of the press. One at a time. It was a job of such monumental tedium, so exhausting physically and mentally, it is difficult to convey. He survived it with a dish of glycerine for his sore fingers and a bottle of Old Grand Dad (tucked between his knees) for his sore spirit.

Twenty years later, I was standing at a cash machine at the Chemical Bank on Broadway and 57th Street, making a withdrawal, when a car swerved suddenly to the curb and a large black man got out and came straight toward me. I was (to my everlasting shame) alarmed until he stuck out his hand and grinned. It was Brooks. We talked for an hour about the *Gazette* and about Eddie Pazant, another Beaufort native, who had gone on to be a first-chair soloist for Lionel Hampton and then formed his own band. (Joe Frazier, the former world heavyweight boxing champion, is another Beaufort native. This is the sad legacy of segregation: during our formative years, we were denied social intercourse by a system that was born of slavery, denied the joy of exchanging ideas at such a young and exuberant age.)

But if Howard Cooper held onto a nickel like a cat with a fresh shrimp, he was progressive. Shortly thereafter, he built a new building just off Boundary Street and ordered a new press, a webfed press! The papers would come off rolls, just as they do on the big-city dailies. Brooks's eyes glazed with anticipation.

One day Howard called us together to announce that the new press had arrived. We all piled into cars and raced out to see it. There was an 18-wheeler backed up to the loading dock. Howard threw open the doors of the truck, and there was our new press: in about 2,000 rusting, worn pieces. He'd gotten it from some defunct Catholic printing house in New Hampshire.

Well, he was partly correct: it was new to us.

Howard hired a retired chief pressman from *The State* newspaper in Columbia to come down and put the puzzle together. The first thing the old man did was lay newsprint all over the floor of the plant. Then he and a helper took each piece and washed it in solvents to get rid of the years of accumulated rust and grease and laid them all out on the newsprint. After the main frame was erected, he would walk around until he found what he thought was the right piece, and he and his helper would go try it.

Eventually it was assembled, and we thought it was real progress. Eventually Howard scrapped that press and bought a new (brand-new, this time) Goss Community offset press. Then we knew we had arrived.

These were financially precarious times for Jane and me. She even ran a small, unlicensed day-care center for a few children. But we lived in an apartment in the basement of one of the grand old houses at 1203 Bay Street, where you could sit out on the front terrace in the cool of the evening. The apartment was decorated with reproduction art ordered from the Marboro discount bookstore in New York. The lady upstairs got *The New York Times* Sunday edition a week late and then passed it on to us—with the puzzle worked. This apartment was our version of Bloomsbury and Greenwich Village (we yearned for New York; I was an early subscriber to *The Village Voice* and a charter subscriber to *New York Magazine* when it started up). A big Saturday night was a six-pack of Pabst's beer (the cheapest you could buy) and spaghetti and garlic bread for whoever showed up. You were lucky if you got more than one beer. For whatever reason, we attracted a small "salon," to which came the likes of my friend Pree, by then teaching English at Beaufort High; Howard Farmer (ex-everything you can name, from radio announcer to real estate tycoon and now a film critic for a newspaper on Hilton Head Island); Norman Spell, who had come down to open a news bureau for *The*

News & Courier; and Hugo Hoogenboom, son of a Dutch father and English mother who owned Beaufort's only bookshop and office supply store. My debt to all is immeasurable, but especially to Hugo. He was a brilliant young man who had gone to Deerfield Academy and Washington & Lee University, ultimately getting a law degree. Between college and law school, he served as a translator and interrogator for U.S. Army Intelligence (he had learned Chinese at the Army language school in California and added that to his fluency in English, Dutch, and French). Pree and I read novels and poetry and discussed them. Howard and I argued movies. (Jane had an extraordinary memory for the most obscure character actors.) But Hugo came over with a Modern Library edition of Plato's *Republic,* and we got down to the serious gaps in my education.

26

In 1961, I was offered a job at *The News & Courier* as an outdoor columnist and general sports reporter. We pulled up stakes in July of that year and settled in the bottom half of a house in Mt. Pleasant, a suburb of Charleston just across the harbor.

Writing the hunting and fishing column was, for me, Nirvana. My father was moderately dazed by the very idea: go fishing and get paid for it. He must have thought about that a lot. (He had served on the South Carolina Board of Fisheries, but that had to do with policing commercial boats.) My very first column began: "Frankly, I'm a fisherman . . ." Uncle Boots quickly involved me in his circle of friends (as did Cousin Pete, who was now an Episcopal minister serving small parishes in the Lowcountry and whose parishioners included many landed gentry with the best of dove, quail, and duck hunting; Uncle Boots by then also was an owner of Tibwin Plantation up near Awendaw).

There were other writing chores (I also covered local high school athletics and those at The Citadel), which I did not mind, except my old nemesis, baseball. Charleston had a

Class-A (Sally League) farm team which played in a battered old stadium out near the municipal zoo. I dodged the bullet (writing about baseball, that is) for as long as I could until one day Warren Koon, the executive sports editor, said, "Look, kid, you're low man on the totem pole, it's your turn in the barrel. There's a doubleheader Saturday night. Be there."

On the appointed evening, I drove out to the ball park and took my place in the press box. The only other reporter there was a local radio and TV sportscaster who did the play-by-play and doubled as the official scorer. It was a sultry July night, oppressive with the advent of rain. The game started, the infield bright under the lights, the luminosity falling off out toward the perimeter. A couple of hundred fans sprawled around the bleachers, sucking on cans of beer and soft drinks and praying for a breeze. The lion in the zoo coughed, his basso voice rumbling across the grass and clay. I settled in to do penance. In the middle of the second inning, one of the most vicious thunderstorms to hit Charleston in centuries (or, surely, it seemed) inundated the city. The games were washed out. I drove happily back to the office and wrote a brief story to that effect. Warren Koon never made me cover a baseball game again.

My father was happier now than I'd ever seen him, even though his grandchildren were a good two-hour drive away. He came to Charleston as often as he could, at least once a week, bade Jane and me affectionate hellos and then took the girls out for a drive. And, when we could, we went fishing. Sometimes he'd trailer the Thompson up to the Ashepoo and I'd meet him. Or, we'd go down to Beaufort for a few days and we'd spend them, more often than not, patrolling our favorite creek or testing the surf at Hunting Island. Moreover, he was due to retire in December, on his birthday. No man ever looked forward to retirement more than Daddy. At last he would be unfettered from the necessary evil of having to work. He would fish. And he would spend time with his grandchildren. But mostly he would fish.

On Saturday, August 19, 1961, a scant four months before his retirement, he complained to Mother that he was not feeling well. She drove him to the Beaufort Memorial Hospital where they checked him in and put him into a room. As they were waiting for the doctor, he turned to my mother and said,- "Darlin', I feel funny all over."

She went to get the nurse. When they returned, he was dead.

BIMINI, *April 29, 1987* —The sun rose over Pigeon Key and the mud flats and mangroves beyond and infused the islands with its satiny pink light. The trades, as if in autonomic response, began to stir the palm fronds desultorily. There was the promise, implied, of langour. I ate breakfast with John Clemans, my fellow angler for that day, and then we strolled down the dock to join the crew aboard *Moppie*, a 50' Bertram. Already aboard were our hosts, Wes Dickman and Jill Shave of the Bertram Yacht Company. We could feel the weight of the heat on our skin.

Ours was one of the last boats to depart, but it did not concern us. This is one of the niceties of fishing along the edge of the Great Bahama Bank: the fishing grounds begin immediately beyond the reef that guards the inlet separating South Bimini from North. Six or seven minutes of coasting through the no-wake zone along Alice Town's waterfront (on the north side), a heady five-to-ten-minute sprint south along the beach to clear the coral and sand blockage, and a sharp turn to the west brings you to the edge of the Gulf Stream. It is here, where the turquoise of the Bank begins to dive into the cerulean deep, that the marlin, the sailfish, and the giant bluefin tuna forage.

As we passed the jumbled docks and dwellings of the village, we could see school children ambling with the slinky fluidity of youth down the dusty Queen's Highway. In the childrens' wakes trailed remnants of the island's dog population, a canine group so inbred that, like Galapagos finches, it has developed characteristics (including personalities) that seem unique.

I stood on the bridge next to Pierre Pierce, *Moppie's* skipper, and wondered what Daddy would have thought of this boat. In his lifetime, he never made as much money as this machine cost. I wondered, too, how he would have reacted to this kind of fishing, where a serious angler/owner easily could spend $25,000 a month campaigning such a boat (considering upkeep, dockage, fuel, bait, and crew salaries). I had said something once about my ambitions to catch the giant billfish of the oceans. (I was much under the influence of Hemingway and Zane Grey.) He snorted in derision. What, he wanted to know, was wrong with catching trout? Nothing, I tried to explain, it was just that . . .

I let it drop.

Once we were around the tail end of the reef, Pierre cut the throttles and the boat mushed into the confused chop. Pierre came nimbly down the ladder from the bridge and his wife Anita, who also is a licensed captain and shares duties with Pierre, ascended. We had a good quarter of an hour before the start of this, the third day of the Big Game Fishing Club's championship tournament and Pierre leisurely began to prepare the baits.

He placed two Spanish mackerel on the outside, or long, lines ("Hell," Daddy would have said, "you could eat *those*.") For the short lines, he used two smaller baitfish, the common balao—prounounced (and usually written) "ballyhoo". Pierre held up one of the ballyhoo and squeezed it, forcing a muddy substance from its anal vent. "Hoodoo," he grinned.

Precisely at 8:30, the committee boat radios that fishing

has begun for the day. Pierre flung the baits overboard and Anita advanced the throttles, bringing the boat up to a seven- or eight-knot speed.

Pierre adjusted the lines so they trailed in our wake at varying distances. I had an ephemeral glimmer of the little Thompson splitting the dark waters of the Combahee, our lines astern, flashing lures tumbling in the black water, trolling for shad. But I was having trouble envisioning my father sitting here in the fighting chair. Oh, he would have tried this. But would he have liked it? (How many angels can fit on the head of a pin? I gave up on theology a long time ago. Why should this worry me? *I* like it.)

When Pierre was satisfied, we settled in for the wait. I took position on the cockpit drink cooler, where I could watch the baits and any movement around them. Big-game fishing accurately has been described as hours of tedium punctuated by moments of pandemonium. When the strikes come, they usually come with little or no warning and everybody—captain, mate, and angler—must be prepared to spring into action. It is a quick, sometimes short-lived ballet, a *pas de quatre* (in our case) that must be performed precisely or the fish will be gone.

I began to sing quietly to myself: "Oh, fish, won't you bite on my line . . ." I could hear Daddy's mellow baritone. It was a short tune. Those were the only words that I knew. It was an invocation, something he had made up. Since his death, I have never gone fishing without invoking it—or his memory.

John Clemans and I have decided that I will take the two left rods, he the two on the right. At some point, we agreed, we would change. An alternative method would be to have one angler in the cockpit at a time, rotating on an hourly or half-hourly basis. But we both want to be in the cockpit and active—active being a relative term. What we must be now is patient.

Patience.

It is assumed and regularly postulated that patience is the forte of all good anglers. It is the reason why many people don't like fishing: the idea of sitting or standing for hours on end without result is anathema. A young academic I met recently said his father had taken him trout fishing and he hated it. "Why would I want to spend hours working to catch a fish smaller than my dick?" he asked. I had no rational answer. Fishing, like prayer, is essentially irrational—unless you're hungry or want a favor from God.

How then, my father? The smallest bird's nest in his line could send him off in a fury of foul language and fidgety gesture. But he would endure a sleeting northeast wind for hours to float his live shrimp over the oyster reefs, perhaps for naught. He didn't care. He didn't mind at all. He was having fun, goddammit. He was.

Pierre likes a clean wake ("So I can see the baits better," he explains) and sometimes will run the Bertram on only one engine, alternating throughout the day. The only disturbances besides the froth churned by the big bronze wheels are created by the teasers, a "daisy chain" of artificial squid towed behind a Boone Bird—a wood and metal gizmo that looks like a half-model for a small nuclear submarine and which flutters and sputters on the surface. Some of the traditional bass fisherman's tactics are at play here: that is, that fish are attracted to signs of distress in smaller fish.

Daddy would have understood this part and liked it.

Pierre has determined that we will spend our day fishing a lazy ovaloid course to the north and back, sometimes taking us within sight of Great Isaac Light, and when we make our turns, the tufted fringes of the Biminis swing by as if on a compass card. The depth here is somewhere between 600 and 1,500 feet. In the middle of the stream, which technically is called the Florida Current at this point, the depth drops to 2,600 feet.

By noon the heat is oppressive. The trades have lain down almost entirely, and the ocean is an oily slick. There is always the seven- or eight-knot apparent wind created by the boat, but none of it is felt in the cockpit. Ironically, on the bridge and in the shade of the hardtop, it is quite cool, and whoever is there must wear a jacket or windbreaker.

Pierre cranks in the bait on the Right Long and examines

it. It is beginning to disintegrate. He replaces it with a two-pound bonefish.

"Change sides for luck?" I query. John Clemans acquiesces. We trade positions in the cockpit. I examined the two rods there and thought about the split-bamboo surf rod and the cobia. It made me smile. ("Great God, boy, don't give him any slack. . . . Hold on to him, Boots, hold on!" Who would be my Uncle Boots here if I were lucky enough to get a strike? Wes, I supposed.) With the minute change in perspective and the added attraction of a new and different bait, we are momentarily rejuvenated, our interests piqued. It does not take long for the somnolence to settle over us again.

At 12:48, John Clemans's head snaps toward the wake. "Fish!" he yells. John (a senior editor at *Motor Boating & Sailing* magazine) is a former charter boat skipper and an experienced spotter, but there is no *sangfroid*—calculated or otherwise—in his voice. It carries the lilt of excitement, and I look immediately where he is pointing. A bill saws up from the sun-struck water behind the bonefish bait on the Right Long. My side. My line. My bait. My fish.

One quick stride across the cockpit, and I am standing next to the chair, my left hand cupping the top of the reel, my right hand ready to come back on the drag lever—which is in the strike position. Pierre comes sliding down the bridge ladder like a fireman.

"Come on, you sonofabitch . . ." He is talking to the fish.

I feel the adrenaline surging into my system.

Again the fish comes up behind the bait, and we see the bill quite clearly and a glint of a great eye. Marlin, when excited, "light up" as the fishermen say; their skin takes on a rich luminescence; the blues and blue-greens positively shimmer. This one looked like a Broadway marquee.

"Come on . . . come on . . ." Pierre and I are chanting together, teeth clenched.

Three weeks earlier, we had had a big marlin come up behind the same bait position and make pass after pass, only to drop off finally without trying to take it. Pierre later remarked, "That fish had 'Pierre' right across his forehead . . ."

And added ruefully, "Only, I didn't see that right under that was 'Fuck you!'"

A third time, the fish lunges toward the bait. We can see its pale blue mouth agape. On the bridge, Anita is cooing encouragement.

Suddenly the fish swipes at the bait and knocks the line from the "clothespin" in the outrigger.

"Free spool!" Pierre screams.

I drop the drag lever back and feel the line streaming off the reel under my fingers. It makes a sound like kittens spitting. Unlike smaller, more sophisticated bait-casting reels, the heavy-duty big-game reels have no worm gear and level-wind to distribute the line and there is no antibacklash mechanism. You use your fingers—with a glove. I had not bothered to put one on, and the line quickly begins to burn my fingertips. It was like that first trout at Whale Branch, only much worse.

We watch the froth of water where the bait had been a moment before. We get a quick glimpse of bill—now pointing away.

"Strike!"

I flip the drag lever up to the button that stops it at a preset tension and yank back on the rod. It shudders in my hands.

"Strike!"

Again I snatch the rod back, planting my feet on the sole and using my body weight as well as biceps in the effort to set the hook.

"Strike!"

Again.

And once more.

And then I hold the rod and feel the savage frenzy at the end of the line. (Godamighty, maybe this is what that pike felt like to Granddaddy at the end of that thin cane pole . . . but magnify it, magnify it . . .)

"He's on! He's on!" I yell back at Pierre.

There is a scramble to clear the cockpit, to bring in the other lines so they won't become entangled in the one with the fish. While Pierre, John, and Wes struggle to do this, I duck under the rod and slide up on the slick polyurethaned seat of the fighting chair and discover that several things that should have been done earlier have not been done: the backrest of the chair had been removed and a custom-designed bait-prep board put in its place, the edge of which now cuts into my back, and the footrest had been shoved up into its shortest position to make walking around it easier; my knees are doubled up under me.

I lift the rod from the side gimbal, and it is almost jerked from my hands by the fish's powerful struggle. With some difficulty, I fit the notched butt into the gimbal between my legs and feel reasonably secure for the first time. And, for the first time, I can concentrate on what the fish is doing. Line is racing from the reel at an alarming rate, making that staccato buzzing sound, a zzzzt . . . zzzzzzzzzt . . . zzzzzt . . . that anglers hear in their fondest dreams and in their most anxiety-laden nightmares. The first jump is short and hard.

"Holy, Jesus, what a fish!" The exclamation seems to come from all of us at once.

The fish jumps again, heaving its massive body above the sundazzle and crashing in a spume of spray. And again it comes up, this time with a prolonged series of lunges at about a forty-five-degree angle to the boat's transom—and very far out. Much too far out for comfort. It does not engage in the spectacular display of smaller, more athletic fish such as sailfish or lesser marlin, which sometimes will erupt and fly across the surface in sinuous *entrechats* that the anglers call "tailwalking." This fish is too big for that. It is capable only of disengaging itself momentarily from the sea and shaking its head ponderously in anger or fear. It is said that the truly giant fish, such as the black marlin off the Great Barrier Reef, can kill themselves, crushing themselves to death with their own weight during these violent maneuvers.

This is what we wait for. This is why we do it. Good weather or bad, big fish or little, it is this moment, the triumph of atavism, that fulfills us. It was always the simple act of being with him, of sitting in the little Thompson and holding a rod and feeling the fish through its tender conduit, hearing his excited encouragement, that was transcendental to any schism that ever was or could be. He might well have denigrated the sheer embarassing expense of spending so much money in pursuit of a creature that is fairly low on the food chain for human beings, unless you were truly hungry. On the tables of the very rich, marlin appear mostly as toothpick-speared, smoked hors d'oeuvres, as if the mighty beast has been deconstructed to tiny building blocks. But, at this moment, he would have thrown arch suspicion of such waste aside and would be following Pierre around the cockpit, in lockstep, just as he had with Coach Small. The only thing that would have mattered to him was that I was catching a fish.

Somebody wrote that we go fishing just to be able to tell stories about it. My father never did. Never wrote a word, never sat around a cabin drinking with a group of his peers, bragging about The Big One. I cannot imagine his having a stuffed sailfish over his desk. His smile in the lemon kitchen light while he held up a good trout was all. And, after supper, he'd say to Mother, "Claire, that was delicious." To which she would reply, "Wasn't it?"

I have also read many times that Hemingway's fishing stories were deeply metaphorical. Hemingway wrote in a letter: "There isn't any symbolysm (*sic*). The sea is the sea. The old man is an old man. The boy is a boy and the fish is a fish. The shark are all sharks no better and no worse."

He also said (to George Plimpton in *The Paris Review*): "The most essential gift for a good writer is a built-in, shock-proof shit detector."

Daddy would have liked that.

I feel a sudden release of pain as the bait prep station is removed.

"Lift your butt," Wes Dickman commands.

I lift and he slides the padded "bucket," a special seat-within-a-seat that allows you to use your legs, rather than your back, to pump the fish up. I clip it into place, snapping the lanyards onto the reel's special rings. (No one but the angler is allowed to touch rod, reel, or line, under rules established by the International Game Fishing Association.)

"What about the footrest?"

"Too short."

Wes makes the final adjustments as I continue to struggle with the bucking rod. To the world at large, there might be some truth in Samuel Johnson's apothegm: "A fishing rod is a stick with a hook at one end and a fool at the other." Not to me. Not to my father. Not to those bonded to me in this battle.

"God, she's a big fish," I say. The fish is "she" now. We have gotten a good enough look to estimate that it will go well over 300 pounds, probably a lot more. The big ones are all females.

"Let's try to get some line back!" I yell up at Anita. Wes is standing directly behind me, guiding the chair, keeping the rod and me pointed at the fish at all times. I can feel his breath on my neck. I also can feel the cotton T-shirt sticking to my body with sweat. There is no wind, and I am haunted by the ghosts of my uncles and my father trailing me around the shrimp boat while the cobia had its own way.

"Glove," Pierre says.

I hold out my left hand and he tries to fit a sopping-wet cotton glove. It is too small. He curses and goes away.

"Come back slowly!" I yell to Anita again.

We hear the big marine gears change, and the boat trembles, shakes as Anita eases forward on the throttles. The blunt transom pounds into the sea, kicking up curtains of spray. The water is deliciously cool, but I have already tasted the salt of my own sweat.

Anita backs in short bursts, and I reel frantically to keep up.

"Hold it!" I yell. Pierre raises his hand and repeats the command.

The timing is good because the fish has decided to swim strongly in the direction of Florida. There is nothing I can do but sit and be patient and watch the line go out. As long as the fish is moving, she is using up strength. I used the moment to extend my arms, especially the right one, and limber it up. The summer before, I had taken two marlin in one day without such preliminary exercise and suffered the consequences: for nearly six months, I could barely lift my arm, much less hit a tennis ball or swing a golf club. It is a soreness of the rotor socket of the shoulder, an injury common to many athletes, especially baseball pitchers. (Are you listening up there?)

Pierre comes back with another glove. It, too, is too small.

"Jesus Christ!" he mutters. "Godzilla. We've got Godzilla aboard."

The third pair I manage to cram my fingers into.

"Would it help any if I told you I'm wearing size 13 EEE shoes?" I tender.

While the fish is moving, I rest. With a fish this size, you let it work against you and the boat, an Iron Woman towing a locomotive with a leather strap in her teeth.

I take off the clicker on the reel (it is used to let you know that line is being stripped), and now we can hear only the line as it goes out, an eerie, strained twanging, like a rubber band being stretched to its limits. Anything—a piece of flotsam, a curious shark—could slice the thread that links us, Moose and me. (Pierre has given her a name.)

A flying fish, alarmed by the boat, flicks its tail and becomes airborne on wide pectorals. It hits the line and slides down it like a circus acrobat. My heart stutters.

An hour after hookup, we begin to make some progress. The fish is still swimming and it is deep, but I can feel that its head is no longer turned away from us. I begin the pump-and-reel sequence, raising the rod until it is vertical, watching the tip until it, too, straightens out, and then quickly dropping the rod and reeling frantically to gain a yard or two of line. I have to do this many times, and two painful blisters begin to swell, one on the inside of my right thumb, the other on my right forefinger. Pierre finds me another glove. The sides of the reel are searingly hot.

It is difficult to tell how closely we can bring the fish before she spooks and swims away again. It is dispiriting to see ten to fifteen minutes of work wiped out in one strong surge as she turns and runs.

Nevertheless, we are making progress, and finally the rigger mark (a piece of dental floss wrapped around the line where it is held by the clothespin on the outrigger lanyard) comes up, disappears in a frenetic burst of fright, comes up again. Now, suddenly, we see the double line. It, too, goes. This is repeated again and again. But, every time, we feel we are winning. Pierre is standing next to the rod tip, moving crablike to one side or another as Wes turns the chair to follow the fish's unpredictable swirls. He is ready to "wire" the fish—i.e., grab the leader. As he stands there, he goes over the gaffing sequence he wants Wes and John to follow. Excitement is building. My muscles are sore, but my energy is renewed. This is the most critical time of all. One mistake—and all of our work, our hopes and aspirations, vanish. It happens more often than we like to think. Most fish are lost right after the strike or at the boat during attempts to gaff them. This is also the time for potential injury. Excited or enraged billfish have been known to ram the boat (it is claimed that a swordfish once penetrated more than an inch of steel hull)—or the man holding the leader. John recalls a mate whose hand was pinioned by a bill.

How many times did my father yell at me: "Don't horse it in! Goddammit! See that? You lost it right at the boat! Jesus H. Christ, son, don't horse them in!"

Don't yell at me, goddammit. Where are you now that I want to be with you so much? You didn't even get to know your grandson and our namesake. On the other hand, you didn't have to witness the wretched tragedy of the breakup of my marriage to Jane—all of it my fault, as anyone could have predicted. (Jane's mother actually did.) But then you also didn't get to meet Robyn, who loves to fish. You two would have been kindred spirits. Once, during our courtship, she and I were standing on a narrow suspension footbridge over the Upper Delaware River. It was a cool September bell jar of an evening. Smoke rose from distant chimneys in straight plumes, and a dog's bark carried from hill to hill. Below us, in the burbling current, some sort of hatch began, and the trout were rising to it.

"God," I said, "what wouldn't I give for a fly rod!"

Robyn looked at me as if I'd finally, irrevocably lost it.

"Fly rod?" she asked. "How about a stick of dynamite?"

You would have laughed as hard as I did.

Twice I actually get the swivel to the rod tip, and Pierre leans over to grab the leader. And twice she lunges away.

"Let her go! Let her go!"

Finally she comes up to the left corner of the transom, a gray-green apparition wallowing sideways in the muttering wash. Pierre takes one wrap around his arm and backs up, drawing her close and making room for Wes to step in with the big gaff. And, when she is struck, she pounds her tail against the boat and yanks the gaff out of his hands. She swims 10 yards away, the silvery handle sticking up like some obscene banderilla.

Pierre beckons to Anita to back down again, gently, so as not to run over the line.

This time the fish comes up tail first. She is exhausted. I bring her head up and get her parallel to the boat, and Wes strikes with the second gaff while Pierre strains against the leader. The fish bursts away, dragging Pierre and Wes across the length of the transom, their knuckles scraping along the gel coat. Together they manage to pull her in tight against the boat again, and John Clemans grabs the rope from the first gaff.

Now, with overpowering brute strength, they bring her back across the stern to the tuna door, a special hinged opening in the transom.

I sat transfixed at the sight of her.

"You can get out of the chair now, Roy," I heard Anita say. "Your job is done."

The fish must have sensed something when she felt the hard heat of the cockpit sole against her body. There was one heaving twitch, and almost instantly the color faded from her as if a switch had been thrown inside. The brilliant rich neon melted to a somber brown. It is the same with all fish: the trout I caught in the French Broad, the trout at Whale Branch, the puppy drum in the surf at Hunting Island. It is odd and humbling to see so graphically, at such proximity, the extinction of life.

The first gaff, although it had struck deeply and left a hole into which you could stick your fist, had come out and ripped off a patch of skin a foot square. It was hanging by this. Under the skin, we can see the tough, corded muscle fiber that almost looks as if it were woven. I notice something else: the blood, the thick, deep red heart blood coming out of the gaff hole in her side. Fatigue and the inevitable sadness settle over me, like some postcoital depression. The act is done. We have conquered. We are depleted. But, sooner or later, we will be reinvigorated, because in each act life is renewed—in very different ways, but a renaissance, nevertheless.

We stand silent for a moment, breathless with exertion, enervated by that and the realization that we have succeeded. And then all hell breaks loose with backslaps, handshakes, and whoops of triumph. Pierre is now estimating that she will go well over 400 pounds. I feel badly for John, but he is characteristically gracious about it.

The prospect of a large fish—a winning fish—is still an event in Alice Town, and the docks are aswarm with townspeople and anglers and crews from the other boats. We wait for another angler's fish to be weighed, and then Moose is hauled up from the cockpit and there is a momentary lull in the hubbub as the weighmaster studies the digital readout on the scale.

"Five-five-one," he calls down to the committee and the assembled. There are cheers, especially from the crew of *Moppie.*

Later Pierre brings the good news that she had already spawned.

There were no other large fish taken. There were, in fact, no very large fish taken on the Bahama Bank all that spring, so Moose was not only queen for a day, she reigned over all for the season, winning the Big Game Fishing Club's championship and the Metropolitan South Florida Fishing Tournament's Unlimited Division.

In the late-night drinking in the smoky bar at The Compleat Angler, she will scarcely be mentioned—if at all. They will talk of Hemingway and Glassell and Lerner and of Maudie Lopez, whose 1,060-pound blue swept everything in the 1983 season. But somewhere on the base of a trophy a few spare facts will be recorded and maybe, in some distant time, an angler will pause and read them. Maybe he'll make an instantaneous association, conjuring scenes from his own experience. Maybe he has a son he will bring here. Maybe he is a son like me and will ponder first what his father would have thought.

Would my father have been proud? Oh, yes.

I walked down to the end of the dock, drink in hand, and stared at the casuarinas and coconut palms of South Bimini, black against the orange afterglow and slack in the evening calm. I remembered the first time my father gave me a drink. I wasn't of age yet, but I was a father, too. I couldn't buy whiskey for myself. He came by the little apartment in Beaufort with a bottle of bourbon, and after he played with his granddaughters, we sat on the porch and watched the clouds slide across the veneer of the river, a trompe l'oeil of innocence. We considered the creeks coming out of the marshes and talked about where the fish would be laying. We talked about the effects of a northeast wind on a speckled trout's dim faculties, the relative merits of fishing the last of the flood or the top of the ebb, versus the last of the ebb and the first of the flood (conclusion: the important thing was the tide had to be moving; trout do not feed in slack water), the importance of keeping a live shrimp floating just above bottom, the advantage of a fish-finder rig when bottom fishing with live minnows, how trout, whether true salmonoids or prettily speckled croaker kin, prefer to lie in quiet eddies and have their food washed to them—pour me another drink, son, and not so much water (he hated a weak drink even more than he hated *Time* magazine)—and about the goddamn liberals in state government who were cracking down on fishing from bridges.

I knew then that I had been accepted.

So, this, then, was his legacy, an alignment of personal stars: a taste for good whiskey (unadulterated), an awe for the Georgian and Barbadian elegance of St. Helena's Episcopal Church and John Hardy's spare sermons; an appreciation for Lowcountry culture, especially Gullah; and an undiminished passion for fishing. How many times had I seen him on the center thwart of our old cypress bateau, making the slow, graceful sweeps of oars—and singing:

> "I got a home and a home at last, don't you see?
> I got a home and a home at last, don't you see?
> I got a home and a home at last.
> I got a home in de tall marsh grass.
> I got a home in dat rock, don't you see?"

At just the right juncture, he'd pause and heave a cast toward the rime-encrusted reeds and watch the cork twirl and dive and, in that suspenseful instant, the world existed only then, only there, only for us.

B
ATTAWAY

Attaway, Roy.

A home in the tall
marsh grass.